The Whole Shebang

McDonald's Young Writers

THE PRIZEWINNING COLLECTION

Illustrations by

DONALD TESKEY

THE O'BRIEN PRESS
DUBLIN

First published 1998 by The O'Brien Press Ltd.,
20 Victoria Road, Dublin 6, Ireland.
Tel +353-1-4923333
E-mail books@obrien.ie
Website http://www.obrien.ie

ISBN 0-86278-574-X

1 2 3 4 5 6 7 8 9 10
98 99 00 01 02 03 04 05

British Library Cataloguing in Publication Data
Whole Shebang: McDonald's young writers 4
1.Children's poems, English
2. Children's stories, English
820.8

Typesetting, layout and design: The O'Brien Press
Cover separations: Lithoset
Printing: Cox & Wyman
All applicants have been asked to verify that their entry is an original work.
The publishers accept no responsibility if this requirement
has not been fulfilled.

FOREWORD

The Whole Shebang is the fourth in a series of writings from the hearts and imaginations of children aged 6 to 16 in the Republic of Ireland. This book follows the success of the previous McDonald's Young Writers collections *The Cat's Pyjamas*, *The Bee's Knees* and *The Top Dog*.

McDonald's Restaurants of Ireland and The Irish Licensees of McDonald's are delighted with the response to this year's competition. Since the McDonald's Young Writers Competition began in 1992 the number of entries has risen from 5,000 to well over 13,000. More than a hundred and fifty children have had their stories and poems published, reflecting a broad range of interest among young writers.

This year's winning entries have resulted in another diverse collection of the best of young Irish writers. We feel it is appropriate that royalties from sales of the book benefit the charity Children's Books Ireland (CBI).

This book has been made possible through the hard work and co-operation of the Irish McDonald's Licensees, McDonald's Restaurants of Ireland, The O'Brien Press and the members of the judging panel, particularly Chairperson Dr Siobhán Parkinson.

Malcolm McConkey
Chairman Irish Marketing Core Group

A WORD FROM THE JURY

Well, here it is, *The Whole Shebang*: poems, stories and playlets, by Irish children from as young as five to sixteen and over. Isn't it lovely? Isn't it gas? Isn't it great to be in it, or to know somebody who's in it, or to know somebody whose auntie's cousin-in-law knows somebody who thinks they know somebody who's in it? Isn't it fun, isn't it daring, isn't it exciting to hope *you* might be in it next time?

Grown-ups are always wittering on about Using your Imagination, aren't they, and the Importance of Encouraging Creativity, and they take competitions like this Very Seriously. (You can recognise the ones who take it all Really Very Seriously because they nod a lot and make notes and keep using mysterious words like 'developmental' and 'enrichment'.)

But we know better, don't we, we writers and readers and kids (and a few of us people that grew up by mistake, while we weren't watching). We know it's really all about having a bit of a laugh, knocking a bit of fun out of writing, and the joy, the *rapture*, of seeing your name in print. Yeah!

The thing is that, unknown to the Very Serious sort of grown-up, kids actually *enjoy* words and rhymes, telling stories and cracking jokes, making daft things up and working out madcap plots and funny characters and surprise endings. It's only when Very Serious grown-ups start worrying about their Reading Age (what a daft-sounding idea!) and whether they're watching too much TV (another idea grown-ups seem very fond of!) that kids start to get scared of the idea of reading and writing.

But, hey, we're not scared, are we? No! Because we know it's really all about having fun with words and ideas.

And now, dear reader, it is your turn, you lucky, lucky person, to join in the fun, and read *The Whole Shebang*. Enjoy!

Dr Siobhán Parkinson
Chair of the Jury

Contents

Puppy

GREGORY MIMNAGH-DUNNE

Puppy puppy,
With your ears so fluffy
and your tail so waggly too,
I bring you for a walk,
Even though you can't talk,
You know I love you.

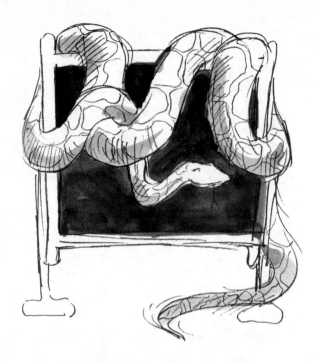

Pauli the Python

LARA CASSIDY

Pauli the python snake ate rats,
Very unusual for a snake.
I always thought they ate Maths,
But I suppose that's an adder,
Because he eats sums and things like that.

The Wrong Parcel

J E N N Y   M c C A R T H Y

One glorious sunny day in Heaven, God sat back in his deckchair, drinking a pint of Guinness and reading the latest copy of *The Daily Cloud*. He personally hoped no-one expected him to appear in a vision right then, or wanted his presence at a wedding. He just wasn't in the mood.

'Excuse me, God?' said one of the young cherubs. 'A parcel has arrived, perhaps it is the new angel?'

God reluctantly got up from his comfy deckchair and followed the cherub to the arrivals lounge.

'God, sir, glad you're here. These parcels just arrived,' said Jim, one of the airport angels, adjusting his halo.

'Good,' God said simply.

Jim led him to the parcels. In one parcel were packets of new bronze slippers for the cherubs, in the second was a new robe for God, himself, and last there was a parcel saying 'Handle with Care'. Jim opened the last parcel and gasped. 'Oh sir, you will never believe what's in here.'

God looked and stood back with surprise. 'Jim, he is one of them,' he said, pointing towards the red-skied land where serpents, winged goblins and other horrible things lived. That place was Hell.

After a while, the creature was sent to the holy quarters. God prepared himself and quickly sprayed on a blast or two of Lynx. The archangel arrived, looking as holy as ever and clasping the certificates in his hand. 'God, sir, let the ceremony begin,' he said.

They went to see the creature. Some hymns were sung and prayers were said. Then God blessed the creature and spoke to him privately.

'So what type of "angel" are you, Satan?' asked God, who secretly knew from experience that he was a devil.

'Well, I try to be as bad as I can and do evil and cause cruelty and grief to others, and of course I help plot to destroy Heaven, that other place near here.'

'Well, you are in Heaven now,' replied God, smiling.

'Really?' said Satan, swinging his tail. 'It's really cool here. Could I stay, please?' Satan sounded as if he had a very bad throat infection.

'Well, we will give you a trial run and see how you get on,' said God.

'Great, thanks,' Satan choked out.

'We really must get you something for that cough,' said God, smiling, as the two walked to the playground.

*   *   *

The playground was a lovely place for cherubs and young angels to play. There were cloud rides, a pond, a cloud-ball court for the older angels, swings, a shoot slide, the flying frame, the chatting  chairs and lots more. Satan looked around and ran over to the other angels who were playing on the swings. They stared at him and started asking him questions.

'Who are you?'

'Do you come from the bad word place?'

One angel, called Karen, started telling the others that he was a devil and he had come to kill them.

God gave out to her about that.

Otherwise, though, Satan had a great time in Heaven.

*   *   *

Satan had a family in Hell, you know, and they wanted to know where he was and what he was doing. So one day his brother wrote a letter and delivered it. It read:

Dear person in charge of Heaven,

We are very worried about my brother being in your hands. We would like him back now, or else we shall start a war. Do as I say or else,

Satan's brother,

14 de Vil Mount Drive,

Hell Hill,

Hell

Satan was not pleased at receiving this letter. He had changed his ways and he had made friends in Heaven. He begged God to hide him. So God brought Satan to his bedroom. Satan crept in amongst the robes and garments and hid there while God went out to meet his parents.

Satan's parents arrived on a raincloud, waving their forks madly and shouting some very rude words. The archangel ushered the angels back to the playground.

'Where is our son?' yelled the parents.

'He wants to stay here and learn good ways,' said God.

'Well, he has to learn bad ways to be a devil, that is his future.'

Then Satan came running out. He had drunk some holy water and was now an angel.

'This is your son,' said God. 'He has chosen his own way.'

With more cursing and swearing, the two devils flew away and all was well. Satan lived happily in Heaven and got a degree in literature.

On the Moon

K I L L I A N   D O N O V A N

One day my friend and I decided to go to the moon. We got some boxes, and then we made a spaceship. It was yellow with blue stripes. Then we painted some pictures on the wall and one of those pictures was a computer.

I pressed one of the buttons and then the magic began. We shot into outer space. We could see the moon and huge craters.

Suddenly we felt a big bump and we were on the moon. We decided not to get out because we had no space suits. But we looked out the window and saw a big eye looking at us. We were very brave. We did not panic, but we pressed another button that made us go back to Earth.

We told Daddy about our adventure and he said, 'What silly children, you saw the man on the moon!'

Hippopotamalla

BRÍD FAULKNER

'Do you remember Africa, Molly?
And our feet in the river muck,
Rolling in slime,
Sleeping 'till tea-time,
And the water that tasted of duck?'

'Do you remember Africa, Molly?
Do you remember Africa,
And the blotting,
And the dripping,
And the spotting,
And the spitting,
And the squashing,
And the squishing,
Along the Muckissippi?'

'Do you remember Africa, Molly?
Do you remember Africa?'

My Sisters

CONALL McNAMARA

I have two sisters, they drive me crazy.
Boy, but they are really lazy!
Barbie dolls and dancing shoes,
Frilly dresses and yuckee foods!
Fighting with me,
Stealing my toys,
How I wish girls were like boys!
Spice Girls, make-up and high heels galore;
They are really such a bore,
I am my mum's darling son,
Pity there is only one!

Lost

SUZANNE CARTER

Lost in the forest, all alone,
Not a person in sight
Or a house for miles.

Suddenly, a creaking,
A crunching, a crackle.
I looked around but all was still ...

Not a person in sight
Or a house for miles.

Quickly, a grabbing,
A pulling, a screaming.
I looked around but all was still ...

Not a person in sight
Or a house for miles.

Suddenly, a stabbing,
A murder, a death.
But no looking around,
Just blood on the ground.

The Secret

KAREN CLARKE

Little Katy lived in a cottage in the woods with her mum and dad. Every morning Katy's dad dressed in his suit of armour and went off to work with his armour lunch box. Every evening Katy's dad came home. Over tea he told Katy and her mum about his day. He told of fighting dragons and rescuing princesses from evil enemies and wrestling with wild wolves. Katy's dad worked as a knight at the castle. Katy loved hearing about her dad's exciting day. She sometimes wished she could fight dragons too. Katy had a plan.

One morning, when her dad left for work, Katy left a note for her mum and crept out the back door. She followed her father from a distance. Katy's dad went through the woods, over the bridge and across the fields to the castle. Katy had to run to keep up. Her dad was inside the castle now. She followed him down a long corridor and down some stairs. She caught sight of him behind a door. Katy went in. Her father's face went red when he saw her. He had an apron tied around his waist.

He explained: 'A long time ago, your mum fancied a flashy knight named Kevin. The only way I could win her over was to pretend to be even more flashing. So I made up stories about fighting dragons and saving princesses. It all got out of hand and I couldn't admit the truth – that I am a washer-upper at the castle. I wash dishes for a living. I've been dressing up in armour and pretending to be a knight for her ever since.' Katy's dad was blushing. Katy decided to keep his secret.

Katy and her dad started washing dishes together. Katy's dad washed them and Katy dried them. They ate lunch and headed for home. They

went across the fields, through the woods and over
the bridge. They were nearly home when suddenly
they came face-to-face with a fierce dragon.

Katy did the first thing that came into her head.
She pulled out her dad's lunch box and threw it at
the dragon's ugly head. It hit him right between the
eyes and made him dizzy. Then Katy stamped on
the dragon's feet. It made him hop up and down like
mad. Katy's dad pulled the dragon's tail. That made
him wail with pain. Then Katy kicked the dragon's
bottom. The dragon quickly ran away. Katy enjoyed
that. She and her dad walked merrily home down
the lane.

Katy told the story over tea. Mum said, 'Well done.' After tea, Katy and her dad did the washing. Katy's dad tucked her up in bed. Mum came in later to kiss her good night. Katy's mum said that she knew her father washed up at the castle and he never fought dragons in his life. 'It is true,' said Katy. Katy nodded off to sleep. She dreamed of fighting dragons.

Tigger and Goldie

LAURA BARRISCALE

I love my two goldfish,
They swim around and around;
My Dad took me to buy them,
They only cost one pound.

I call them Tigger and Goldie,
They're the best of friends, you see;
Tigger is nice and stripey
And Goldie is glittery.

They don't cause any trouble,
They're as quiet as can be;
I watch them blowing bubbles
As they're looking out at me.

I wish I was a goldfish,
At swimming I'd be good;
But I'd have to change back at dinner time
'Cos I don't eat goldfish food.

Ted

J E N N I F E R   H E N R Y

I have a dog,
His name is Ted.

I love to kiss him
And rub his head.

His coat is black,
His feet are white.

He barks at me
To say good night.

Domhnach is Dálach

SEÁN Ó LOINGSIGH

'An bhfuil éinne ansin?' a ghlaoigh an seanbhacach, ag suí suas díreach. D'éist sé go cúramach, ach níor chuala sé ach na tonnta ag bualadh ar an trá. Shocraigh sé síos arís ina scáthlán truach; long adhmaid bhriste, seacht dtroigh déag ar fad. Chaith sé seanchóta dufail donn a bhí caite is lán de phoill agus chlúdaigh seanchaipín caite a shúile. Dhá pháipéir nuachtáin seachtain as dáta, a d'úsáid sé mar bhlaincéid, agus leag sé a cheann aosta siar ar sheansac a bhí dubh le salachar.

D'éirigh sé óna phrochóg ar bhreacadh an lae, agus scuabáil sé chuig an líne lán mara agus bhailigh sé adhmad farraige chun tine a lasadh. Timpeall leathmhíle síos an duirling rith an Abhainn Dúnfhinn isteach san fharraige. Thaistealódh clann ealaí síos in aice leis an trá agus thabharfadh lucht saoire bia dóibh. Bhí seanaithne ag an mbacach agus ag na healaí ar a chéile, agus ag a leathuair tar éis a seacht ar maidin thiocfaidís ar snámh, dhá eala óga ar téad. Cleite óg liath chocánach a chlúdaigh an dá eala óga, agus gob giortach a bhí orthu. Chlúdaigh brat cleití comh bán le sneachta an gandal. Lena mhuinéal suas díreach sheas sé aon slat in airde. Gob fada a bhí aige, agus é dubh ar a bharr. Bhí cleite níos dorcha ar an mbaineannach, ach bhí siad fós chomh hálainn leis an eala eile. Roinn an bacach cúpla píosa aráin leo sular chas sé i dtreo an bhaile.

Ní cathair ollmhór a bhí inti, ach don seanbhacach, a bhí cráite le hairtríteas agus daitheacha agus gach saghas rud, thóg sé tamall air aon fhad a thaisteal. Shiúil sé go cráite trí na sráideanna, ag stopadh gach deich gcéim le haghaidh sos a ghlacadh sula rachadh sé deich gcéim eile, agus sos eile a ghlacadh ansin. Go mall agus go cúramach dhreap sé céimeanna oifig an phoist agus bhailigh sé a phinsean.

Lean sé ar aghaidh ar a thuras mall saothrach go dtí gur shroich sé teach beag ar an taobh eile den chathair. An tÚllord an t-ainm a bhí ar an teach. Bean aosta a bhí ina cónaí ann. Duine cineálta a bhí inti, agus bhí miongháire le feiceáil ar a haghaidh bhog rocach i gcónaí. Bhí stábla beag aici ag bun a gairdín. Bhí dath donn air agus doras dhá chomhla. An t-aon áitritheoir den tigín sin ná seanchapall 'Clydesdale' nach raibh spraoi ar bith fágtha ann. Donn dorcha an dath a bhí ar a chóta, agus moing fhada dhubh a bhí air. Ní raibh sé úsáideach a thuilleadh, ach lig an tseanbhean don bhacach aire a thabhairt don chapall. Thug sí cúig phunt dó gach seachtain; ní go hiomlán don obair a rinne sé don chapall, ach mar thrua dó.

Ghlan sé amach an stábla, d'athraigh sé an tuí

agus thug sé bia don chapall. Ansin thug sé uisce nua dó, agus thosaigh sé ar an gcapall a chíorú. Chuir sé blaincéad ar an ainmhí, dhún sé an doras agus d'imigh sé leis. D'fhág sé slán ag an tseanbhean ag an ngeata agus bhuail sé amach i dtreo na trá.

Thóg sé a chuid ama, ag dreapadh céimeanna beaga tríd an bhaile. Chas sé cúinne agus shiúil sé síos bóithrín beag clúdaithe le clocha duirlinge garbha chuig an trá. Bhí an ghrian ag dul faoi, agus chonaic sé na healaí ar snámh i bhfad uaidh, ag gluaiseacht i dtreo na habhann. Chuaigh sé anonn go dtí an long bhriste, agus d'fhág sé carn beag de pháipéir nuachtáin istigh ann. Bhí an tine a las sé ar maidin múchta dár ndóigh, agus bhailigh sé cúpla cipín eile. Thóg sé bosca lasán brúite as a chóta agus las sé tine bheag. Shuigh sé síos os comhair na tine ar feadh tamaill sular chas sé ar ais chuig an long. Shocraigh sé an sac agus leag sé amach na páipéir nuachtáin mar bhlaincéid.

Luigh sé síos ina long bhriste, ach shuigh sé suas arís agus ghlaoigh 'An bhfuil éinne ansin?' D'éist sé go cúramach, ach níor chuala sé ach na tonnta ag bualadh ar an trá.

The Big Spaceship

MICHAEL REIDY

Once upon a time there was a big spaceship. It was so big that a whole town's worth of people could fit in it. One day some very stupid scientists thought they should send a town to space, just for a laugh.

And so they did. They packed everything in the town – a zoo, a shop, three hundred cars and all the people in the town – into the spaceship. When everything had been packed in, off they went to the launch site.

The count down began: Ten, Nine, Eight, Seven, Six, Five, Four, Three, Two, One, Blast Off!!! There was a puff and a cough and a bang. It was broken. After all that work and all that packing the spaceship was broken. One of the scientists went under the spaceship to see what was wrong. Then there was a loud blast. The ship took off into the sky. After it did the scientist came out frazzled to the bone. He looked up at his friends and then he dropped on the ground.

Meanwhile, inside the spaceship, the people and animals were barking and yelling at their success. 'We're off! We're off!' They shouted.

Then someone spoke up: 'Er, wait a minute … where are we going?'

'We don't know,' they all answered. And the fact was that they were going to the sun! They figured that out after they looked at the charts. 'Hey!' someone said, 'look at this, these charts say we are going to the sun!'

Everyone started to panic. 'We're gonna die!' they shouted, 'Help us! Help us! Somebody help us!'

'Hold on,' somebody said. 'Calm down, it's just a matter of steering us around.' They went to the control room, but to their horror there was no steering wheel. Everyone was gobsmacked. They looked at each other and then at the empty place where the steering wheel should have been. The spaceship was being controlled by a remote back at the launch site.

Back at the launch site all the scientists were drinking water. All of a sudden one of them spilled their water on the machine. The machine exploded. The controls broke. The spaceship never came back to earth, and for all I know it could still be drifting in space.

Jackpot

M A R I A   M E A L L Y

Model's legs, yeah right, the only thing that Loeletta Demont has are spots and cellulite. I made my way to the Chantell model agency, not ever thinking that I would be picked for the running five top young models for *Mizz* Magazine with my braces, wispy, mousey hair and the face of a bull's behind. But I was trying and trying to get a shot at fame in the endless fashion parades of Gucci and Prada goods. I should have waited until my three-inch glasses had been replaced by beautiful contacts, and a wig if I was lucky.

Anyway, I made my way to the huge gilded hall of the agency, not even caring if one part was dedicated to recovering half-men half-chickens, or circus acts that have been out since 1890. Even if I did have discharged teeth I would give it a shot. The high vertical stairs were the biggest I had ever encountered, and I was welcomed by two old women who smelled of sheep manure and cow vomit. They had purple highlighted hair and even the clothes they wore smelled like regurgitated mouse droppings. I was confused. Just for the sake of fun I asked them if they had seen a herd of cows nearby, or whether it was in their handbags.

I had a feeling that today would be my lucky day. Maybe if I took off my glasses and took my hair down I would pass for a *Mizz* model. I stuffed my bobble into my bag and placed my fragile glasses in their leather case. A big door opened smoothly and I walked in. You know that feeling when you think everyone's looking at you, and you try to look cool? Well that's how I felt – nervous, and even a little scared that I would be thrown out for insulting those women and men.

I tried to clear my throat and said aloud, 'I am Tina, Tina Henderson, em … I want to audition for the *Mizz* model photo shoot. The other girls in the room looked at each other and started to snigger. I felt so embarrassed and humiliated. The time had come to make a swift exit as I knew that nobody would be interested in photographing me, even if I did have straight teeth. I ran down the stairs with a lump in my throat the size of Alaska.

I decided that now was the time to make my statement – to take my braces off, push in my contacts and give my appearance a good shopping spree.

Three months down that road of shops, orthodontists and opticians I finally had the appearance of a confident, well-dressed, attractive teenager. Boys were swooning around me, as I now had blond hair, had lost three stone and my contacts were firmly fixed. The thing that I loved most about not having my braces in was that I didn't have to wear a bib to eat spaghetti. I could also read a paper without bringing it up to my chin.

The minute that I was ready for that second audition for *Mizz* I was gonna knock 'em dead. Now I would dress to kill, and when I arrived in that hall where I was three months before, I would be on their list to be photographed for *Mizz*.

The lead man was a tall, tottering man with a brown suit and snowy grey hair. He looked dodgy and seemed to be the leader of the gang. Nobody dared to cross him or talk back. The woman in the corner was the head chooser. There was a lot of politics floating around the room. I walked in and walked up to the woman, saying in my head, I will succeed, I will.

'I am Tina Henderson, here for the audition for *Mizz*. Here are my photos.' She looked impressed and that was a boost to my self-esteem, which was now at an all-time high. Not even the stuck-up girls in the group near the window would ruin my jackpot, and my jackpot was to become a model. Even my mother, who was previously a protester in the trees of the Phoenix Park, trying to save the squirrels, said that I would become successful as a small-time model.

'Maria Jameson, Paula Simpson, Lily McGuinness. And the last name on the list is …'

I was sweating like a dog and I suddenly felt a

chill through my spine. Was this the chance I was waiting for, with all my money down the drain on tight skirts and flares, black dresses and contacts? Was this the end of my jackpot, my dreams, my goal? Here it comes, the last name, all hope is gone, there's no turning back. If I lose I will never breathe again, what will I do? Those two minutes felt like a lifetime. This was my only hope, my chance to make it big.

'... Tina Henderson.'

Was it me? Was it me? My name? It was and I would be famous – every girl's dream, my dream, my jackpot.

Lá Mór a Bhí Agam

P Á R A I C   Ó   h É A N N R A I C H

Lá amháin, chuaigh mé féin agus mo Dhaidí go dtí Old Trafford agus lá an-mhaith a bhí againn. Nuair a shroicheamar an t-aerfort ag Manchain, bhí cara le mo Dhaidí ann chun sinn a thabhairt go dtí an teach lóistín.

Nuair a shroicheamar an teach lóistín, chuireamar ár málaí isteach sa seomra agus ansin chuamar go dtí staid Old Trafford. Nuair a shroicheamar an Iarsmalann, bhí an treoraí ann agus thug sé sinne agus cúpla duine eile ar an gcuairt. Chuamar ar cuairt na staide ach ní rabhamar ábalta dul isteach go dtí na seomraí feistis mar bhí sé ródhéanach.

Chuamar amach chuig an staid agus ansin thosaigh an cluiche. Tar éis cúig noiméad bhí Manchain Aontaithe ag buachaint a haon a náid agus ag leatham bhí siad ag buachaint a ceathair a náid. Ag leatham chuamar isteach agus bhí deoch againn agus ansin chuamar amach go dtí an staid. Nuair a bhí seachtó nóiméad imithe bhí sé a cúig a náid agus ag deireadh an chluiche an scór a bhí ann ná: Manchain Aontaithe a seacht agus Barnsley a náid.

Tar éis an chluiche chuamar chun deoch a ól. Ina dhiaidh sin chuamar amach chun na himreoirí a fheiceáil. Bhíomar ródhéanach chun chuile dhuine a fheiceáil. Chonaiceamar Ryan Giggs agus Olé Gunnar Solskjaer.

An oíche sin chuamar chuig an bpictiúrlann chun *Men in Black* a fheiceáil. Nuair a bhí *Men in Black* críochnaithe chuamar ar ais chuig an teach lóistín.

An mhaidin dár gcionn d'éiríomar agus chuamar chuig an aerfort agus fuaireamar an t-eitleán abhaile.

Nuair a shroicheamar aerfort Bhaile Átha Cliath, bhí ár ngluaisteán ann agus chuamar abhaile. Bhain mé an-sult as an deireadh seachtaine sin.

Fireworks

SINÉAD FORDE

They sizzle like hot sausages
Frying in a pan.

Then they burst into a million pieces
And different colours collide.

Yellow, blue, orange, red –
All make a different pattern.

Upon the night's black wallpaper
They burst and then die down.

A Day in the Life of My Dog!

ORLA LOUGHMAN

It all started on a sunny Saturday morning. I went to Funderland with a couple of friends. When we were inside, Triona spotted a new tent. 'Madame Lopaz' it said, on a board overhanging the entrance. Rachel explained to me that Madame Lopaz was a fortune teller and if you paid £1 extra you could have a wish. I decided that I would go in, pay my pound extra and see if my wish would come true.

I entered cautiously. The tent was circular and draped in red, with gold tassels hanging here and there. Suddenly there was a loud bang and in front of me I saw what must have been Madame Lopaz. She beckoned me forward with one finger. 'You would like a wish,' she whispered mysteriously, with her middle finger and thumb on her temples. I could not help grinning because the woman looked like a psycho from a horror film. The so-called woman gave me a nasty look so I stopped grinning.

'Tell me your wish,' she hissed.

I pondered this carefully. If I could wish for anything in the world ... 'I've got it. I want to live in my dog's body for a whole day – twenty-four hours,' I exclaimed, regretting at once what I had said (I would have preferred some chocolate sweets). I was about to ask if I could change my wish, but Madame Lopaz had disappeared. I stumbled out of the tent, dazed.

Rachel, Triona, Barbara and Sheila crowded around me. They questioned me about it: 'Was it good?' 'Did your wish come true?' 'What did you wish for?' and so on. I don't know what I said, and I don't think they understood what I said either! When I arrived home I felt very strange. We played until seven o'clock and then I said goodbye to my friends and had my dinner.

I woke up the next morning beside the radiator in the hall. I stood up and stretched. Everything looked different. Why did I wake up beside the radiator? Then it dawned on me. My wish had come true! I tried to look at my hands but when I moved them I collapsed onto my tummy. Then I saw my hands, but they were *paws* and had black, shiny hair on them! I decided I'd have preferred a box of chocolates. That reminded me, I was hungry.

Suddenly the ground shook. 'Oh no, an earthquake,' I thought, but it was John, my brother, pounding down the stairs like an elephant.

'Come on, Cinders,' he said to me, 'come and get your breakfast.' What? The cheek of it! I followed him anyway because I thought it would be nice to have some food. He took a can of dog food out of the fridge and told me to fetch my bowl. I ran off obediently to find it and returned in a flash. I saw him dig into the dog food and dump some of it in my bowl. He put the bowl on the ground. I looked at it in disgust. There were brown and yellowish lumps still in the shape of the can in the bowl. Yuck! John bent down and affectionately told me that I was the stupidest mutt he had ever seen. There are some people I just cannot bear, John being one of them! I pushed the bowl away with my paw. It takes some getting used to, being a dog.

I noticed that one of the presses in the kitchen was open. It was the sweet press. I was in luck! I trotted over gleefully. A box of jelly babies lay on the bottom of the press. Perfect! After I had gobbled down all the sweets, I walked clumsily into the sitting room. The couch looked comfortable so I jumped onto it. Then the ground started shaking again and my other brothers and sisters pounded into the kitchen. My mom walked into the sitting room, saw me and shouted the following (by the way, I'm leaving out the bad words): 'Get down off my good chairs, you mutt.'

Having recognised the look she was giving me as murder, I jumped off the couch and fled out of the room. I went to my bedroom and lay down on my bed. The big teddy that I had got for Christmas was taking up half the room on the bed. I felt very squashed. For the whole afternoon I dozed, until I was woken by Dad coming home from work. I ran down the stairs. Gosh, I thought desperately, I really need to go to the loo! Where am I supposed to go? Outside! I ran to the back door and started scraping it. Dad saw me and opened the door. When I had finished my business, I trotted back in and to my surprise Dad called to me.

'Yes, I'll take her to the vet now. I can't understand why she didn't eat her breakfast,' my Dad was saying to my Mom. What? He can't understand me not eating that disgusting muck? He wouldn't like to eat it either, so why do I have to go to the vet? These thoughts came rushing through my head all at once. Then Dad pushed me into the car and drove away from the house quickly.

Now I know what dogs feel when they go to the vet – sheer panic. Waiting in line was the worst of all. I know, because when your owners start talking to you in a voice as pure as chocolate (and that's pure), you know something bad is going to happen. When we were finally allowed in, the vet took a look at me and said, 'She needs an injection.'

What! Did I hear wrong? Injection? No way! I thought. I hopped off the table and ran for the door. I never made it to the door, but I did a bit of fighting and then I realised, 'I can bite!' The realisation came out as a long bark, which I think the vet mistook as a war cry. Anyway, I lost and that was the last thing I remember until I woke up the next morning in my own bed. Back to normal at last! The next thing I thought about was that if Funderland was still open I could have another wish. However, Funderland had closed on the eighth of January. That was yesterday.

The next year I visited Funderland again, but the man in charge told me that Madame Lopaz had left. Well, that was the end of that but I am still a bit puzzled. What I want to know is: who was in my body when I was in my dog's?

The Purr-fect Catwalk

STEVEN MARKEY

Purr-fectly walking
On soft velvet paws,
Purr-ading the catwalk
On stiletto-like claws.
Stretching and pawing
And purring with glee,
She yawns as she softly
Jumps onto my knee.

Her almond-shaped green eyes
Blink with content –
All the time she spends grooming
Is time really well spent!
Her soft, gleaming fur coat
she has licked at for hours
While she lay sunning herself
On top of Mum's flowers!
She won't get in trouble
For the damage she's done,
She'll just miaow and purr
And rub up against Mum!

She'll cast yet another spell
... Kapow! Just like that,
Mum's fallen in love
With Porsche, our cat.

Uaigneas

MAIRÉAD NÍ
CHOISTEALBHA

'Is seanbhean mise anois a bhfuil cos liom san uaigh agus ceann eile ar an mbruach,' mar a dúirt Peig Sayers. Tá mé in Áras na Seandaoine agus táim anseo le deich mbliana ó fuair m'fhear céile, Seán, bás. Nuair a fuair Seán bocht bás ní raibh sa teach ach mé féin agus dúirt m'iníon Máire liom dul isteach san Áras. Nuair a chuir Máire san Áras mé d'imigh sí léi go Meiriceá agus ní chastar thart í ó bhliain go bliain.

Tá na daoine san Áras an-dorcha agus dá bhrí sin bíonn an-uaigneas orm. Tá na cairde uile a bhí agam sa bhaile básaithe nó róshean chun cuairt a thabhairt orm. I rith an lae léim an páipéar nó breathnaím ar na carranna ag dul siar agus soir an bóthar.

Nuair a dhúisím i lár na hoíche bím ag smaoineamh ar an seansaol agus ar an gcraic a bhíodh agam féin agus ag mo chairde. Ach mo léan, tá an lá sin caite anois agus táim anseo san Áras gan chara, gan chompánach.

Uaireanta, cuirim an raidió ar siúl ach tá mé bodhar agus bíonn na daoine san Áras ag casaoid go bhfuil sé ró-ard. Is mar sin a chaithim an lá san Áras gach uile lá.

Dinosaur Land

KEVIN O'REGAN

My name is Kevin. I am a Diplodocus Dinosaur and I live in a cave in Dinosaur Land. Some dragons were breathing fire at my family and because I found this cave and took shelter in it, I am the only surviving dinosaur in Dinosaur Land. Here is my story:

I lived with my Mammy and Daddy in a different cave, with all my dinosaur friends. Every day we would eat lovely green, juicy leaves which we pulled from the pineapple trees with our mouths.

When we played we had great fun. We played squash, monopoly and numba-rumba. School was not invented yet. We learned how to fight, and to stretch our necks to eat leaves from the trees.

One day I saw fire coming over the hill. I was frightened, because I did not know what it was. Then I saw green wings coming over the mountains. It was the dragons and they were breathing fire at me. I ran into a new cave. I was afraid the dragons would breathe fire into the cave, so I ran into the back. Then I was safe.

Then, when the dragons went away to find more dinosaurs, I came out of the cave. I saw all the dead bodies of my dinosaur family and my friends.

This is a new day. I am on my own. Now I have to start a new life. I am sad that I have lost my family and old friends, but I hope that I will find more dinosaurs around the parts of Dinosaur Land that I haven't seen yet. I am glad that I am alive.

The Kill

GAIL CUMMINS

Along the walls and sills she prowls,
    Waiting for the kill.
A shadow in the peaceful night,
    She spots her prey and stills.

Her back is arched, her ears alert,
    Her eyes a swirl of light.
Attractive, yet a beast to some,
    A creature of the night.

A chilling growl from deep inside,
    The rodent turns in fear.
It stares its captor in the eyes,
    Knowing death is near.

She then sits back and eyes her toy,
    Displaying fangs with glee.
The rat, now overcome by fright,
    Bolts towards a tree.

The cat is strong and glides with ease,
    The rat is short and weak.
When close enough to get a grip,
    She pounces on her meal.

Though many beasts can see this plight,
    It's none of their affair.
For animals must eat to live,
    Just as they breathe the air.

The rat, now pinned upon the ground,
    Awaits his gruelling death.
As claws like knives sting at his throat
    He draws his final breath.

Now, contented with her catch,
    She creeps back to her lair.
And settles down to sleep in peace,
    Her stomach no longer bare.

Rampaging Rimmer

JAMES DUFF

Hi, my name is James Duff and I come from a family of four. My best friend Niall went on holidays to France and asked me to mind his hamster for him. As I have never had a pet of my own I was really looking forward to minding Rimmer, as the hamster is named. The only thing that was standing in the way was Mum and Dad.

Convincing Mum and Dad was harder than I thought. 'You've never had a pet of your own before,' Mum said. Whose fault is that? I thought to myself. 'I don't think you are responsible enough to mind a hamster,' said Dad. After much begging and grovelling they finally decided I could mind Rimmer. I couldn't believe it, my very own pet for two weeks.

Niall brought Rimmer over the day before he went away. Rimmer was brown and white with tiny ears, black beady eyes and two vicious-looking teeth. He was deadly looking. Dad said I had to keep Rimmer in my room. I asked Niall would that be all right. Niall grinned and said that would be great. After he had gone I couldn't help wondering why Niall had laughed at the idea of Rimmer staying in my room.

That night I made sure he had clean water and plenty of food before I went to bed. Two hours later I realised why Niall had laughed – Rimmer only came out at night! Swinging up and down, running round and round in his wheel and climbing up the bars of his cage he made a terrible racket all night. I couldn't help but notice that he resembled a miniature Arnold Schwarzenegger!

The next morning when I awoke Rimmer was fast asleep. 'Huh! It's well for some,' I said to him. I had only had two hours' sleep and when I came down

Mum took one look at me and said, 'I hope you were not up half the night playing with that hamster.' I just mumbled something and promptly fell fast asleep, head down in my cornflakes.

Rimmer turned out to be a very interesting pet. When you gave him his food he would fill up his mouth so much that the sides of his neck would swell up until he looked like a balloon. Then he would go to a special place in his cage and spit it all up, to Mum's absolute horror. She nearly had a heart attack when he did the same thing with his bedding.

She came tearing down the stairs, screaming that Rimmer was choking. But I explained to her that that was the way he made his bed. She swore she never wanted to set eyes on him again.

When Rimmer had been with me for three days I decided to clean out his cage, as there was a bad smell in my room and Mum was not happy. So I put him into the laundry basket and left it in the garage while I set about the dirty task. But then I decided to watch a football match on TV with Dad. When it was over I went to get Rimmer but he was not there. All sorts of thoughts were running through my mind – he could be sizzled to death in the electrical box, getting washed in the washing machine or being dried in the tumble dryer! I started searching frantically through boxes of toys, clothes and shoes, but to no avail. Rimmer was gone.

I sat down and tried to work out what to do next. I wondered if I could get another hamster like Rimmer in the local pet shop. Just then Mum came in with Rimmer in her hands. I could not believe my ears when she said she had felt sorry for him in the laundry basket and had decided to let him out for a little run around the garden. He had had a great time. Despite giving out about him at first, Mum was now fussing over him like a new baby! I was really glad to have Rimmer back, but it didn't last long, as Mum now took over minding him full-time and I did not get a look in.

When Niall came to collect Rimmer, Mum was very upset and the next day she went out and bought a pet hamster. Maybe the next time I get to mind someone else's pet it will be a dog and who knows? Mum might just get to like it too.

If I Had Three Wishes

MARK O'REGAN

I wish I had never been born. Everybody in St Peter's Secondary School teases me about my hair, my hurling skills and even about the poor state of my house. One day, on my way to school, I found a *sliotar* with loose sewing. I had my hurley with me so I took it out and I hit it along the ground three times. Then the ball split and a puff of smoke rose into the air. A genie appeared and offered me three wishes. There were two rules. They were (1) I could not wish for more wishes and (2) I could not reverse any wish. Then the genie disappeared. I thought it was a joke. Smoke could affect my asthma, I thought to myself, so maybe I'd imagined it all.

That afternoon I had hurling practice. I wished to myself that I was the best player on the team. Guess what? It worked! While I was the same as always, everyone else had become terrible. They couldn't play for a million pounds. I knew just how terrible when I hit the *sliotar* to Bill, who was usually the best player on our team, and he missed it and it hit him in the face. 'Yahoo!' I cried to myself, because I was now the best player in the school. I was off the hook – no-one would tease me about my hurling skills now!

The next day I wasted wish number two. I was eating in the cafeteria when Bill came along. He dropped his lunch purposely on top of me. Everyone laughed. 'Oops,' laughed Bill. I knew he was clumsy, but no-one could be that clumsy. My best clothes destroyed! My mum would have a cow. I was so upset. I said, 'I wish everyone would get lost.' That instant everyone disappeared (I found out later that they were wandering the Sahara desert). I could not believe my eyes! I rubbed my eyes hard, so hard it hurt.

I ran from the cafeteria through the empty school, down the empty road and all the way home at top speed. 'Mom! Dad!' I shouted, as I raced into the house, but there was no answer. 'Nooooo!' I roared, as I rushed around the house. I was on my own. After a while I calmed down – after all, I still had one wish.

That night I was tossing and turning, and I could not get to sleep. I kept thinking about the last wish and what it should be. The next day, after a lot of

thinking, I made wish number three. I wished I had every computer and all the computer games in the world. I am a bit lonely now but do you know what? I think I am beginning to enjoy my cool new life and when I want a normal life, I can always wish upon a star, can't I?

Childhood Pastimes

A I S L I N N   F L A H E R T Y

Fill bowls of water
And leave them there,
Wet my teddies
And cut their hair.

Play with my dinner
And wrestle my brother,
Trap flies in jars
And let them smother.

Juggle with oranges,
Paint on the windows,
Tickle Mum's toes
And make houses with pillows.

[No characters in this are fictitious.]

No Exit

A O I F E   C A H I L L

Here I am in my own personal prison, chained to the wall. My prison has no door and no window, just four walls. It's almost as if it was built for me. Maybe it was. Since I opened my eyes and had the strength to move I've been testing the walls for weaknesses, kicking and pummelling them as hard as I can.

Even though there are no doors, hatches or windows to put food through, I never feel hungry. There must be something wrong with my memory because I cannot remember anything before waking. Since then my eyes have adjusted to the dark and I can see quite well. I notice that even though I wear no clothes, I feel no cold. My prison is like a hot-water bottle, always warm.

I think that my captors like to torment me, as I can hear muffled voices outside of my prison. Sometimes they laugh and sometimes it is as if they are talking to me. The walls of my prison seem to be closing in on me.

I am beginning to grow lonely. I have no-one to talk to or to interact with. The muffled voices are becoming clearer and I can understand some words. I call to the outsiders but they do not answer. I am desperate to be released. There seems to be no exit!

The walls have stopped closing in on me and I find it easier to move around. My chain is lighter now that I'm used to it. I'm growing frustrated and I flail at the walls in vain. 'I want out!' I scream. My tormentors tease me with silence.

I hear a noise. It sounds like a drum. Lub-Dum, Lub-Dum, Lub-Dum. It beats constantly. This sound moves around. It's very near now but I cannot pinpoint it exactly. Something brushed up against me. There is someone else here! Now that we have met I do not feel lonely any more. Although we don't speak the same language we communicate using gestures. Sometimes both of us pound the walls until we exhaust ourselves.

Tonight I was awoken rudely. My friend was already awake. Suddenly a door opened and gloved hands pulled my friend from our prison. I heard cries of pain and anger from outside. The hands came for me. I was pulled roughly into the outside world. The pain was excruciating. I was held upside down and thumped on the back. I screamed. Somebody wrapped me in blankets. I was placed on a bed between my sister and my mother. I had been born.

Ag Fanacht

M A R I A   N Í   D H U I N N Í N

Tá seachtain amháin eile fágtha againn,
Aon chéad seasca is ocht n-uaire,
Táim ag crith le háthas agus le heagla,
Níl a fhios agam cad a dhéanfaidh mé.
Hurá, Hurá, tá an lá anseo,
Tá sé leathuair tar éis a trí,
Glaonn an teileafón ar an mballa,
Tá m'athair ag caint go tapa,
Briseann mo ghol orm,
Léimim suas san aer,
Tá deirfiúr bheag nua againn,
Aingeal ó Dhia is ea í.

The Intruder

AUDREY WALSH

The door creaked slowly. I turned quickly, my eyes fixed on the door. I was struck with fear and my heart was beating against my rib cage. It was just the wind. I continued reading my book, even though I really shouldn't be reading horror books. A door slamming upstairs made me jump. I threw some more coal on the fire.

Then I heard footsteps coming down the stairs. I stood up straight. The stairs creaked. There were goosebumps all over my flesh. I turned off the light and tried to hide. The footsteps passed by the door. My heart was in my mouth. Suddenly the footsteps stopped. The door pushed open. Terrified, I held my breath. I could see a pair of hands reaching out for my throat. I screamed.

The intruder panicked and fell over the table in his hurry to escape. I screamed again and again and again. Suddenly all hell broke loose. Voices started shouting out my name. I could hear my big brother thundering down the stairs. I could hear my mother calling out in terror. I felt something brush past me. The pounding in my chest was so loud I thought my heart would burst. I wished I had gone to bed early. I wished it with all my heart – why didn't I do what I

was told? Why wasn't I able to behave? Why did I sneak back downstairs when the lights were out? The TV wasn't even that good tonight. And I had school tomorrow. No – no school tomorrow! I'll be dead by then. Tomorrow they'll all be crying over my coffin! I'll be dead! Stone dead! Died of fright. All Mam's problems will be over. She won't have to shout at me ever again: 'Do your homework,' 'Go to bed,' 'You'll be late for school.' No, she'll have peace and quiet – after she buries me, that is. I screamed again and I began to cry.

All of a sudden the room became bright. The hands were shaking me now – I looked around me. I saw Dad kneeling down in front of me. It was his hands around me – my dad! My brother John was in the room too, and Mam was standing behind him. I looked around. There was no-one else! No intruder! No-one! Dad had gone upstairs when he came home and found my bed empty. So he tiptoed quietly down to carry me back to bed without waking me, not to kill me!

We all began to laugh out loud.

I Remember

TADHG Ó BROIN

I remember the sound of gushing water,
As the kettle was being filled;

The sound of hobnailed boots on flagstones,
As grandfather inched toward the fire;

The sound of crackling turf
And a clink, as the frail man
Placed the kettle on the metal shaft,
Over the flickering flames;

The sound of bubbling liquid,
As the water boiled.

Oh it would put the longing on you
For a decent cup of tae.

Puddin

MICHAEL CALLERY

Puddin is round,
Puddin is fat,
Puddin is my favourite cat.
I feed my Puddin
Liver and milk.
Her coat is soft
And shiny like silk.

One of Those Days

ANDREA   BONNIE

It was one of those overcast, dull days when you would rather die than get up at half seven to go to work. The alarm went off at the correct time, but it was so cold outside and my bed was so snug and cosy I just turned over and went back to sleep.

I woke at half nine, hours late! I was due at the office at nine o'clock, and I had a really important meeting coming up in fifteen minutes' time. I fixed myself up as best I could in five minutes, sacrificing breakfast, and bolted through the door.

My car had frozen over and would not start. Typical! I couldn't find the antifreeze so I decided to catch the bus. As I rounded a corner the bus was just pulling away.

'Wait!' I called, flailing my arms about but, unsurprisingly, the bus continued on its way. Suddenly a car sped by, soaking me from the waist down. I screamed in frustration at the driver, not caring at all who heard me. This was a very bad start to the day.

In the end I walked to work. I was late already so I didn't see the need to rush any more. The insides of my Laura Ashley shoes were sopping wet, because I'd walked through a puddle that was deeper than I'd reckoned.

On arriving at the office building – 157 Upper Conlon Street – I headed for the lifts. I had to get to the twelfth floor and didn't fancy climbing the stairs. I got into the lift and pressed number twelve. This was the first time I'd stopped moving since I'd got up. There was a peculiar smell in the lift, like mouldy bread mixed with sour milk. I held my breath. There was also a demented mother in the lift, with a wailing baby who wouldn't stop screaming. There was another woman behind me who was continuously sneezing, and when I felt the back of my neck it was mysteriously wet. I gave her a look but she didn't seem to notice.

The lift stopped at the ninth floor and both women got out. I let my breath out. The smell seemed to have disappeared, which was a great relief. I was beginning to think that maybe the day wasn't going to be so bad after all, when who should come running towards the lift but Sharon Fletcher!

Sharon Fletcher is the cleaning lady. She's a revoltingly fat woman with hair growing from her chin. But don't get the wrong end of the stick; this isn't the reason why I despise her. She is an extremely nosy, arrogant person and is the biggest gossip I've ever known. She only talks to people to obtain information and spreads rumours and scandal around about everybody. Sharon Fletcher was the last person I needed to see on a morning like this.

'Yoo hoo!' called Sharon, and stepped into the lift beside me. 'You know I was on my way back from getting a nice new packet of J-cloths, minding my own business like, and I said to meself I said, Sharon, are you seeing things or is that Jessica McDonald coming into work at five past ten of a Monday morning? I would never have believed it of you,' she said in a disgusted tone.

'I slept it out,' I answered curtly, not wishing to have any further conversation with the ghastly woman.

Suddenly, without warning, the lift jolted and I

had to lean against the wall to steady myself. Then it simply stopped for no apparent reason. Sharon let out an exaggerated shriek. 'We're going to die!' she screamed dramatically, like someone in the movies.

'The lift has only broken down, Sharon,' I remarked wearily. 'I expect it will be fixed in a few minutes.'

A few minutes later, nothing was happening. I glanced at my watch – a quarter past ten. I sighed deeply. I couldn't stand being stuck in a lift with Sharon Fletcher one moment longer, so I pressed the emergency button,

expecting to hear a friendly voice on the other end. Nothing. This was a nightmare! Trapped in a small, enclosed area with Sharon Fletcher and no contact with the outside world!

The minutes ticked by and Sharon, having overcome her earlier hysterics, now seemed to be enjoying herself and was talking nineteen to the dozen and taking deep drags from a smelly brand of cigarette. '... and then you'll never guess, doesn't she only go and tell her husband! I couldn't believe it meself and you know I'm not the type to judge people, but honestly, I mean the very idea ...' And so Sharon droned on and on and on, waffle waffle waffle ...

An hour or so later the lift suddenly shuddered. I wasn't prepared for it and I toppled over and smashed my head off the floor. The pain was unbearable. And then I saw them – the open doors. They were like Heaven's gates, calling, beckoning to me. I crawled out and escaped from my stifling, claustrophobic prison. I jumped to my feet, forgetting the pain in my head, and ran to the stairs, leaving Sharon still talking far behind me.

I bounded down all twelve flights of stairs, no longer trusting the lift, and ran outside into the lashing rain. Not caring if I died of hypothermia, I ran straight home, not once stopping for breath. I marched straight into the kitchen, leaving a trail of water and muddy footprints behind me, and poured myself a large bowl of Shreddies. I'm not usually one for superstition, but I now firmly believe that if you start your day the wrong way things are sure to get worse.

Having finished my Shreddies I trudged slowly upstairs, beginning to feel the events of the day take their toll. Not bothering to undress, I flopped straight into bed. My boss was going to crucify me tomorrow, but what could I do? On days like this, you're better off staying in bed, so that's exactly what I did.

Inspiration

S O R C H A   M c D O N A G H

Inspiration is hard to find;
        Not on the sofa,
        Nor behind.
Not on the chair,
        Nor anywhere.
It's not in the room,
        Not here or there.
Come on inspiration,
        Play fair!

The Puca

PETER MARTIN

'Every year on 31 October a man screams to wake the dead. First he is put under a trance and the Puca – a tall, ugly demon – chews at his leg until he screams. This scream is not like a scream from any man. The Puca's venom goes into the man's heart and the man's scream is so loud that it wakes the dead.'

My Grandpa finished his story.

'But what has happened to the Puca?' I asked him.

'He was locked away. But they say that every one hun –'

'That's enough,' interrupted my Grandma. 'You'll scare the poor boy,' she added.

'Oh please, Grandma,' I said. 'I really want to hear Grandpa's story.'

'No,' she replied. 'I want to help you make your Halloween costume,' she went on.

'All right …'

That night, Grandpa finished his story. 'As I was saying,' he said, 'every one hundred years the Puca is set free and he finds someone to wake the dead. It was one hundred years ago when the Puca was last out.'

I went to sleep that night thinking about what Grandpa had told me. I was scared.

I woke up the next morning and went into the kitchen, where I found Grandma and Grandpa eating their breakfast.

'Happy Halloween,' said Grandma. 'Today we will make a nice, tasty brack for our Halloween feast.' I love Grandma's brack. It is the nicest I've ever tasted.

'I want you to come with me to John

Armstrong's farm and pick a pumpkin to carve,' said Grandpa.

When we got to John's farm we had a look around until we found a pumpkin the size of a football. We picked it, said thank you to John, and left.

After we carved the pumpkin, I went over to Grandma and she told me to get out the eggs so that we could start baking the brack. When we had put it in the oven I got into my Halloween costume to go trick-or-treating. 'Be back before nine,' said Grandpa sternly.

So off I went to all the houses in the area and got sweets, nuts and things like that. When I came to John Armstrong's house, I found the door open. I called for him but I got no reply. Just then I saw him, looking over at something. I could not see what he was looking at because of the trees in the way. A scream came from him, a loud scream. Then it hit me – the Puca had bitten his leg.

I ran back to my house and told Grandpa what had happened. He ran out to the shed. He came back with a shotgun and we went to the graveyard. When we got there we saw two zombies. 'Stand back,' said Grandpa. Bang! I turned around and saw green slime everywhere.

That night we went around getting people together to stop the zombies and the Puca. All the people of the town met in the town square. Everyone was about to attack when over the

horizon a light came and all of the zombies turned into green slime. And as for the Puca, he was pulled into the ground, not to return for one hundred years.

'You see,' said Grandpa, 'the dead can only stay out on Halloween night. The Puca is let free at eight o'clock and at sunrise he's gone.'

'But what will happen to poor John Armstrong?' I asked.

'I don't know,' replied Grandpa. 'I think he will recover. Now, let's get back home.'

'All right,' I said.

Just then, I opened my eyes and found myself in my bed. I got up and went into the kitchen. The calendar had '31 October' written on it.

'Grandma, did you forget to change the calendar?' I asked.

'No,' she said. 'Happy Halloween.'

An Turas

NÓRÍDE NÍ
MHUIMHNEACHÁIN

Ní dhéanfaidh mé dearmad go deo ar an lá iontach a bhí agam le linn laethanta saoire an tSamhraidh.

Le m'Aintín i Loch Garman a bhí an tsaoire á caitheamh agam féin agus mo dheirfiúr. Oíche amháin dúirt ár nAintín linn go raibh rud éigin beartaithe aici dúinn don lá dár gcionn. Cuireadh a chodladh sinn go luath agus sinn ar chipíní ag iarraidh cuimhneamh ar cad a d'fhéadfadh a bheith ann. Bhí gach sórt smaointe inár gcinn ach ar deireadh thiteamar inár gcodladh. Dúisíodh sinn go luath maidin lá arna mhárach agus d'inis ár nAintín dúinn faoi na pleananna a bhí aici don lá. Ba dhobair gur thit mé i bhfanntais nuair a chuala mé an scéal. Bhíomar ag dul go dtí an Bhreatain Bheag!

Bhí ár ngiúirléidí ullmhaithe aici i mála don lá. Ar leathuair tar éis a seacht d'fhágamar an teach chun dul go dtí Ros Láir a bhí trí mhíle dhéag uainn. Bhíomar in am mhaith don bhád agus chuamar go dtí an seomra suí agus shuíomar i dtaobh an tseomra. Bhí seomra spraoi ar an mbád fiú amháin agus bhí an-spórt go deo againn ann idir liathróidí agus balúin agus sleamhnáin. Bhí an-ocras orainn faoin am sin agus fuaireamar béile blasta sa bhialann. Chuamar suas ar bord chun radharc a fháil ar an bhfarraige. Bhí sceon croí orm nuair a chonaic mé na tonnta móra ag bualadh i gcoinne na loinge. Ní raibh talamh le feiceáil in aon áit agus bhí eagla orm nach bhfeicfinn talamh go deo na ndeor. Ach níorbh fhada go bhfacamar talamh na Breataine ar fhíor na spéire. Bhí áthas orm a bheith slán sábháilte i dtír arís. Bhí saoire iontach againn ina dhiaidh sin agus tharla a lán eachtraí suimiúla dúinn. Ach sin scéal eile ...

Macs 'n' Milkshakes

MICHELLE McDAID

When I am hungry,
Or feel like a treat,
I go to McDonald's
For something to eat.

The staff are so cheerful
While I make up my mind;
While I look at the menu
They are helpful and kind.

I go to the counter
And decide what to take;
I order a Big Mac
And a chocolate milkshake.

For value and service
It's the one place to be –
For my breakfast and lunch
That's where you'll find me.

When you want to meet
All the people you know
McDonald's is the place
Where you should all go.

My Collection of Colours

AILEEN ARMSTRONG

Oh! There you are. I was beginning to wonder if you'd ever turn up. The beach is empty. It's just you and me. Are you cold? A little? Here, take my jacket. I'm as warm as toast.

This is what people might call a grey day, but they're wrong. If they would only open their eyes, they would see the true beauty of the colours all around them. See the sand? It's sloppy and muddy, but it's not just grey. Oh no! Look closer. Bend down, right down.

Now do you see? It's brown, beige, rusty, grey, blue, oh, it's even black in places. It's fantastic! I could do a whole series of paintings just on the sand here.

And don't you dare call the sky dull. It's anything but that. It's early morning here on my beach, my favourite time of the day. It's still quite dark, but isn't this lovely? Navy-blue light is what I call it. What time is it? Eight o'clock? Perfect! We're just in time. Oh, look! The cover of navy blue is lifting! Can you see the layer of brightness underneath it? Can you see the colour slipping along the blushing horizon? The navy blue is fading, fast now – see how a pink colour is creeping in? The blaze is spreading all across the coastline. Oh! The sky is alive, streaked with colour. Bright pink, dusky pink, fiery orange, and the bright glare of winter-yellow sunshine. Shield your eyes, it's strong. And are those clouds orange too? The ones high up in the sky, where there is still a faint wash of navy blue? Yes, they are, pale orange. I can never decide which I like better, pale orange or fiery orange.

Wait! Where are you going? I haven't finished yet, you know. We haven't even started on the sea. I think the sea is my favourite part – so endless, timeless, yet ever-changing. Yesterday morning it was like glass, and I liked it like that. But today – just look at those white horses! Careful now. Step back from the spray a bit. We may get a bit wet. No matter! It's worth it.

The waves are beautiful, aren't they? Yes, you heard me – beautiful! Deep greens and greys. Deep green is such a mysterious colour, I've always thought. But can you see the blue as well? No? Concentrate. The blue shades are gorgeous. Sometimes there are dark blues and sky blues, but this morning, I think it's mostly slate blue.

Look how the waves crash against the shore! Watch how they rise in perfect swells. If my crippled hands could still hold a brush, I'd paint this scene for certain ... Oh! Don't go, not yet! Don't you want to hear more? We're only halfway through! Oh ... well, goodbye then ... if you really must go. It's just

... oh ... it's nice to have someone to talk to. I'm just a lonely old man, really. I'm sorry to have wasted your time. I should probably be on my way, too. It was nice to have someone to share my collection with. My collection of colours, you know. I'm feeling ... rather tired ... goodbye ...

An Bád Bán

EIMEAR O'LOUGHLIN

D'fhéach sí mórthimpeall
    Ar an amharc léanmhar a bhí ann
Daoine gléasta i ngíobail, cnámha ag gobadh
    I líon os comhair an Bháid Bháin.

Atmaisféar gruama is éadóchasach
    Boladh gránna san aer
Rug sí greim daingean ar a beirt pháiste óga
    Is bhreathnaigh sí suas ar an spéir.

Chuimhnigh sí ar fadó
    Ar Ghearóid is a leanbh Eibhlín
Sular tháinig an Gorta is an fiabhras
    A ghoid an bheirt acu uaithi.

Cuireadh iad le chéile gan chónraí
    Sa chluain in aice an tí
Ní fheicfeadh sí iad nó an chluain arís
    Ach bhí na mílte cuimhní aici.

D'fhill sí go dtí an t-am i láthair
    Le tarraingt bhog ar a méar
'Táim ocrach a Mham, is tá tart orm
        chomh maith.'
    Arsa sise, 'Bí foighneach mo stór,

'Táimid ag dul go dtí an Talamh Úr
  I bhfad ón ocras is brón
Tá bia is deoch go flúirseach ansin
  'S ní bheimid i ngannchuid níos mó.'

Ghuigh sí go tostach go mbeadh sé sin fíor
  Is neart intinne ó Dhia a fháil
Dhiúltaigh sí géilleadh, ar son Ghearóid
        is Eibhlín
    Gheall sí a clann a shábháil.

Chuaigh siad ar bord na loinge
  Chun taisteal ar thóir saol níos fearr
Ba theifigh iad anois, cuid den mhilliún go leith
    A d'fhág Éire le linn an Ghorta Mhóir.

A Week in My Life – a Witch's Story

L A U R A   P O W E R

MONDAY: By using my spells I got out of bed and had a lovely breakfast of mashed worms, jellyfish jam and beetle juice. Put on my filthy hat and cloak and flew to the witches' meeting on my broom. At four o'clock I practised my spells for ages. At midnight I went to bed.

TUESDAY: Got up and woke Moon-Light, my black cat. Had my usual breakfast, then had a grease shower and put on some new shampoo which claims it can help to increase dandruff. Practised my magic and told the goblins to shut up next door.

WEDNESDAY: Woke late again and had a grease shower. Bought some water beetles and frogs for my experiments. The goblins still won't be quiet. Went to bed at one AM.

THURSDAY: Woke with a back pain. Quickly eased it with magic. Maybe it was all the flying yesterday. Got my broom to do all the house-work. The goblins were so hungry, they caught Moon-Light on his late-night bog walk. They were just about to put him on the boil when I noticed he was gone unusually late, popped into their cave and saved the day.

FRIDAY: Woke up, flew (on my broom stick, naturally) out of bed and, as I realised the time, magicked my clothes and hat on and went to visit Witch Sharkhaggle. On approaching I saw some bog water for sale and couldn't resist it. When I arrived Sharkhaggle told me I wasn't supposed to visit until Monday but she invited me in anyway. We had more bog water, some green-mould sandwiches and some jellyfish-jam biscuits.

SATURDAY: Woke up to a lot of unpleasant surprises – there was some green glue in my slippers, all my bills had to be paid and, worst of all, my flying licence had run out. I had to wait nearly all day to apply for a new one because the flying centre was run by stupid hobgoblins who thought I wanted a learner's licence. After much explaining I got my licence but as I finally flew home over the trees I fell brutally and sprained my arm. Went to bed and couldn't remember any of my spells.

Nothing to Do with Fish

V A L   N O L A N   (J n r .)

Six o'clock AM: The precise time an exact replica of a 1932 Hawaiian pineapple-shaped alarm clock started to shriek.

Six-o-one AM: The time an exact replica of a 1932 Hawaiian pineapple-shaped alarm clock slid across the floor and cracked the toilet bowl.

Half dazed, Graham crawled out of bed, only to find himself somewhere that resembled the bathroom. Slowly, memories began to flood back to him – eating his home-made duck *à la splot* (or something); two hours sitting on the toilet, working out how to sell VISA cards to eskimos. ('You haven't got one? Every igloo in Alaska should have one of these. How do you de-ice your Husky without it?')

Graham also remembered a questionable decision to move into the bathroom permanently. He vaguely recalled moving stuff in, assisted by two nice masked men who may or may not have taken the television and VCR, carpet, stairs and possibly the north-facing wall (it was getting a little chilly).

Splosh. Splosh. Splosh.

Oh, and the toilet bowl was leaking.

*   *   *

Graham dragged himself up to the door, not daring to look in the mirror for fear of seeing a webbed foot hanging from his mouth. That was, he resolved, the last time he tried out anything he saw on *Yan Can* (or, as he decided, *Cannot*) *Cook*.

Graham Genge was an insurance salesman. Not a particularly inspiring job, but it left him plenty of time to become a bingo-hater and part-time Christmas-tree quality tester. Graham had originally come from Malaysia, from a large Australian family that lived in a Russian ghetto (don't ask, it's complicated). He had never liked Malaysia, and had resolved to get himself an education and leave. He had taught himself two languages before someone told him that Latin and Yiddish would get him precisely as far as the nearest bus-stop. Now he lived in a normal, everyday, semi-detached house, in a normal suburban area, with three of his neighbours' cats and a large percentage of the town's rodent population.

*   *   *

Holding down what was possibly a beak, no, wait … a wing, he made his way, as one does in the morning, to the breakfast table. He opened the door and found himself face-to-face with a strange creature he couldn't readily identify. It was about six feet high and scaly, with very pronounced bones jutting out from over its eyes and a short grey trunk.

It was also helping itself to the contents of Graham's refrigerator.

Graham rubbed his eyes for a moment, hoping to banish the image. When he looked up again the creature was sharing out the remains of the duck *à la splot* with another similar creature.

'Ah,' the first thing said, noticing Graham for the first time. 'Come here, good being, we'll take the amphibian please, and the mouldy cheese-like substance.'

Graham blinked slightly in disbelief. 'I'm sorry?'

The first creature began to look slightly uneasy. 'You are the waiter ... aren't you?'

'Er ... No. Not quite.'

'Em ... This is the Avoeddols III fly-through restaurant?'

'Er ... No.'

'The Treorb VII refuelling port?'

'No.'

'The Astreis II shopping centre?'

'No.'

'The Zirs Prime food hygiene and art appreciation complex?'

'No.'

'Then where ...' He looked at his fellow-being for support, '... are we?'

'You're in my kitchen.'

'More specifically?'

'Earth.'

There were several long moments before anyone spoke. Finally, the first creature put the plate back in the fridge.

'So,' he said at last, 'that would mean that you have absolutely no interest in buying yoghurt.'

'I beg your pardon?'

'You can't have it. It's mine,' said the thing.

'No, no. I mean, why would you want to sell me yoghurt?'

The alien crossed the kitchen and put its arm on Graham's shoulder. 'Put quite simply, my friend ... em ... what's your name?'

'Graham.'

'Graham, mmmm. Can I call you Sam?'

'Well, er ...'

'Great. You see, Sam, yoghurt isn't just yoghurt.'

'It isn't?' Graham asked, already forming an insurance policy around yoghurt in his mind.

'Yoghurt is in fact the meaning of death.'

'It's what?'

'The meaning of death. Believe me, our corporation has spent millions of Galactic dollars. We've had the finest minds doing nothing else but working on it for years.'

'And all you came up with is yoghurt?'

'That's about all. We found some chilli hot-dogs too, but someone ate them.'

'Oh. But if this yoghurt is worth so much, why sell it to me?'

The alien jumped back in mock surprise. 'You don't want to buy?'

'Well, no ... em, I might know some people who might want to buy.'

A small smile spread out from under the creature's trunk. 'I knew we could do business,' it said. With one swipe of its hand, it knocked everything from Graham's table and deposited a large metal suitcase. The case had the words 'Stolen from Navert Bay Fishing Co-op' printed on it. Graham ignored that. The alien opened the case to reveal a fully fitted-out office-in-a-box. The first alien dragged the second, by the trunk, over beside him.

'This is Yifda. He's going to be the area salesman.'

'Hi,' said Yifda.

Graham tried to interrupt, but he was shouted down.

'Yifda has experience in nuclear power plants, collects guns as a hobby and has an interest in curtain design.'

'Oh, that's brilliant,' muttered Graham.

'Brilliant? It's zarping fabulous!' said Yifda.

Graham frowned at him.

'But it gets better. Do you know how to use a telephone?'

'Of course. I'm an insurance –'

'Fabulous.' The first alien grabbed three cordless telephones from the case and dumped them into

Graham's arms. 'You can take all the calls.'

Graham was speechless for a moment, then quickly dumped the telephones and fought back.

'I am not answering telephones or designing curtains or anything like that, 'cause this is my house and I want you out. Now.'

The alien snorted slightly. 'I'm afraid I must tell you, Sam ...'

'Graham.'

'... that this is no longer your house, but the sales distribution node of Galactic Yoghurt Products Inc. Like it or lump it.'

'You make lumpy yoghurt?'

'Only for special occasions.'

Graham paced the kitchen. He felt a slight compulsion to begin tearing his hair out. The managing alien grabbed some notices and began putting them up around the room.

'You can't do this!' Graham shouted.

'Of course I can. I own this company.'

'This isn't a company. It's my house!'

'He ain't heavy,' Yifda muttered in the background. 'He's my brother.'

'This is insane!' Graham screamed.

'Maybe it isn't,' the managing alien said. 'Maybe it's just you.'

'We'll soon see,' Graham replied, throwing the front door open. He took a quick look around the street and found one of his neighbours. 'Hey, Grant,' he yelled. 'Am I crazy?'

The managing alien grabbed Graham and pulled him back inside before he could get an answer. 'Go away,' he shouted across the street. 'We're having a board meeting.' With that he slammed the door with his highly articulate trunk.

Graham steadied himself against the sink. Finally he confronted the creatures.

'Look,' he said firmly. 'I don't want you here. I don't want your yoghurt or your radioactive interior designers ...'

'Curtains,' Yifda corrected.

'So just clear off and leave me in peace.'

The managing alien was silent for a few seconds, then he began laughing. *'You* don't want *us*?'

'Brilliant. Your language skills are something else,' replied Graham.

'Fine. Fine. We'll take our yoghurt elsewhere.'

'And your phones,' Graham replied, kicking them towards the creature.

'And our phones,' the alien snorted, picking them up and depositing them in the case. 'When we're ruling the planet from a partly-skimmed milk-product empire, you won't be getting any employment offers.'

'Fine,' Graham said defiantly. He opened the door and waved them towards it.

'Come on,' the managing alien said, directing Yifda towards two bicycles that had been lying unnoticed beside the washing machine. The managing alien picked up his case and followed Yifda out. Graham was about to shut the door when a lamp-stand that had been sitting in the kitchen corner for years suddenly grabbed what seemed to be its own luggage and followed the hose-heads out.

Graham sighed and shut the door. It was going to be just another tough day at the office. Almost. He found himself a bowl of cereal and sat down for his breakfast. It was only then he noticed the sign on the wall:

MANAGEMENT WILL BE HAPPY TO ENTERTAIN ANY COMPLAINTS OVER A BOWL OF SOUP.

(Noodles Optional)

Graham noticed, with a slight tinge of irony, that quite a lot of soup had appeared in his kitchen, for no apparent reason. He also wondered how two aliens had come fifty zillion light years on bicycles, what the meaning of death really was, and did he really look like a waiter?

'I might call in sick today,' he muttered to no-one in particular.

*   *   *

It should be carefully noted, however, that the morning's events had nothing to do with fish.

Inis Oirr

DIARMAID Ó
hALMHAIN

Árainn Álainn,
Bradáin Bhreátha,
Currach Canbháis,
Duirling Dhorcha,
Eascann Éasca,
Faoileáin Fhiáine,
Gliomach Gleoite,
Happy Hooker, Ha Ha!
Iascaireacht Iontach,
Loch Lurgan,
Mangach Mara,
Neantóg Nimhneach,
Oileán Órga,
Plassay Praiseach,
Ronnach Rúnda,
Seolta Síogacha,
Tonnta Tréana,
Úr-Uisce.

The Spell that Went Wrong

FERGUS MONNELLY

Once, when I was sick, I asked a wizard to cure me. He came over to my house with a big book of spells. He showed me the one that would make me get better and then he left. The word I had to say was 'Ookkaala'. I said it, but I coughed once in the middle of it.

The next day my condition deteriorated rapidly. I wondered had I made a mistake in the spell. I opened the book of spells but before I could find the healing spell I flicked open the death-spell page. It said, 'Say "Ookk", cough once, then say "aala".' But it was the writing underneath that caught my eye. It said that the antidote was not in the book. I jumped out of bed and headed for the phone.

I rang the wizard, hoping he was at home. He answered after three rings. I told him my story and he said he would come over. After a short wait the wizard burst through the door. He wasted no time in saying a spell. Suddenly everything went blurred. When my vision came back everything was huge. Bending down to me, the wizard explained that I would not die, but I would have to spend the rest of my life as a spider.

An Muicín Dána

COLM Ó CUINN

Lá amháin chuaigh mé féin agus mo Dhaidí go dtí an t-aonach i Mám Trasna. Chonaic mé féin an muicín álainn seo. Dúirt mé le mo Dhaidí í a cheannach dom. 'Ceart go leor,' a duirt sé agus cheannaigh sé é. D'ioc sé cúig phunt ar an muicín. Thug muid abhaile linn é agus thug mé cúnamh do Dhaidí é a chur sa scioból. Chuile lá thabharfainn béile agus deoch dó. Lá amháin nuair a bhí muid bailithe go Doire Né tháinig mo chara Seán ar cuairt chugainn. D'fhiafraigh sé de mo mháthair an bhféadfadh sé an muicín a fheiceáil.

'Ceart go leor,' a dúirt sí, 'ach dún an doras i do dhiaidh.' Ach mo léan géar, d'fhág sé an doras oscailte agus d'imigh an muicín amach. Síos leis go dtí an trá. Bhí scoláirí thíos ag an trá ag snámh agus bhí a gcuid éadaí fágtha ar chloch acu. D'ith an muicín na héadaí go léir. Nuair a tháinig siad amach as an uisce ní raibh éadach le fáil, bhí na tuáillí féin ite ag an muicín dána. Bhí siad ar buile.

Chuir an múinteoir fios ar na gardaí, ach níor éirigh leo greim a fháil ar an muicín dána. Ní raibh a fhios ag aon duine cé leis é. Nuair a chuala mise céard a tharla chuaigh mé féin dá chuardach. Fuair mé é, sul má rinne sé aon damáiste eile, agus thug

mé abhaile é.

Maidin lá arna mhárach d'éirigh mé go moch agus chuaigh mé féin agus mo Dhaidí ar an aonach arís. Dhíol mé an muicín dána agus fuair mé deich bpunt air. Go dtí an lá atá inniu ann níl a fhios ag aon duine céard a tharla don mhuicín dána. Ceapann daoine gur shnámh sé go hÁrainn agus ceapann daoine eile gur ith na scoláirí é le haghaidh an dinnéir.

A Normal Day

SINÉAD CAMPBELL

Alva sighed and looked carefully around the playground. Jessica, Lisa and Sandra were not there. They had been bullying her for almost a month now but she was too scared to tell anyone. There was no-one in the playground now, well, unless you counted one or two girls from fourth class. Alva walked cautiously out of the front playground and down towards the gate. So far so good. 'Maybe they have gone home,' she thought. 'Maybe they're going to give up bullying me.' She perked up at the idea. It was a beautiful spring afternoon and that started Alva daydreaming.

'Hey, wimp, leaving so soon?' Alva turned around slowly and saw, standing in front of her, Jessica, Lisa and Sandra. They all had coy looks on their faces and were trying to appear cool. They walked slowly up to her.

'So, how's Mummy's little pet today?' said Jessica in a babyish voice. 'I just love your pigtails and your little bunny rabbits.'

Alva blushed. She had liked this cardigan, it was her favourite, but now she was having second thoughts. 'Oh why didn't I wear my black sweatshirt?' she agonised silently. She looked at the ground, feeling all her courage draining away. At the same time, she felt panic rising in her as she furiously tried to think of some excuse to explain the dreaded bunny rabbits.

'I ... am ... you see I ...' Alva stuttered, 'my mother loves it and made me wear it, you see, it's horrible, isn't it?'

Then Jessica stepped so close that Alva felt her breathing. 'I'm sure,' she sneered. 'Why don't you step into my office.' Lisa and Sandra had made an office-like square with their hands and stood in front of Alva, smiling slyly.

'The office door is open, just step on in,' said Lisa.

'Yeah, step on in,' chorused Sandra. Jessica pushed Alva into the 'office' and started to encircle her. Lisa and Sandra followed Jessica. They started to chant, 'Alva is so boring 'cos her last name is Gorey!' That brought tears to Alva's eyes. She started to tell herself that big girls don't cry, but that only made it worse and tears started streaming down her face.

'Mummy's little baby crying again,' said Jessica in a baby's voice. Then they started to pull Alva's hair and tug at her cardigan and dress.

'Stop, leave me alone … stop it … stop it … stop!' Alva screamed.

'Stop, leave me alone, stop, stop,' the other girls mimicked. Alva regretted shouting 'stop', because then they started hitting her and hitting her hard. Jessica punched her hard on the nose. Alva fell to the ground. She felt a searing pain go through her head. Her body stiffened in a mixture of pain and fear. There was complete silence. Nobody dared breathe, not even Jessica. Alva felt her nose. It was pumping blood.

'You … deserved that,' Jessica said uncertainly. Alva slowly stood up. Jessica, Lisa and Sandra then did the last thing Alva expected – they started to encircle her again and chant horrible, mean things about her. They also started to pull her school bag and eventually they took it from her. They emptied it all over the pavement. After what seemed an age,

Alva noticed that they were taking her stuff.

'Leave the rest,' insisted Sandra. 'What we have taken is all crap anyway. Now let's find out where she keeps all the good stuff.'

'Check her,' said Lisa. They went through Alva's pockets, shoes and everything, but found nothing. Jessica, Lisa and Sandra each gave her a slap across the face, saying that it was for not having anything worth taking.

When Lisa was slapping her, she noticed a string around Alva's neck. They pulled it roughly off her and found a pouch. Inside the pouch was where Alva kept all her valuables.

'Look what we have here,' said Lisa.

'Money, fancy pens and pencils, everything,' answered Sandra.

'You can't keep anything from us,' said Lisa.

'Yeah, we're too good,' said Jessica.

The final outrage was when Jessica took off Alva's glasses, dropped them on the ground and then stepped on them. 'Oops, I guess I broke them. Ha, ha, ha,' she said, laughing.

Alva just wanted to scream and shout at them, to hit them back, in an effort to make them understand what they were doing. All the anger inside her just wanted to burst out. But she wouldn't, she couldn't. She felt so alone. Life was not worth living. What was wrong with her that they had to keep picking on her? 'Why me?' she silently wailed, 'why me?'

'Hey, wimp, we have got to go now, my mom's gonna kill me if I'm late home,' said Jessica coolly. 'But don't worry, we'll be back, we always are.' Jessica, Lisa and Sandra stalked off. Alva started to pick up her books and pens. It was just another normal day for her. After all, she could not tell anyone.

Change

JOHN HOSKIN

Change is something old people hate,
But young people anticipate.
Old people's hate turns to fear
When they hear death whispering in their ear.

Haiku: Alone

CLARE HOLOHAN

The glistening snow
Falls upon my freezing cheeks
Like small tears of ice.

For Your Own Good

ELLIE   FRY

You can't go out like that, dear,
You'll catch your death of cold.
That top looks too mature, dear,
You're just fifteen years old.

Don't use so much make-up, dear,
You'll only make a mess.
That perfume's very strong, dear,
So use a little less.

You can't wear that short skirt, dear,
I can see your underwear.
Please wear some woolly tights, dear,
Your legs look awfully bare.

I'll pick you up at ten, dear,
You can't stay out too late.
You've got to wake up early, dear,
We'll leave for school at eight.

You cannot pierce your ears, dear,
Until you're seventeen.
Never kiss a boy, dear,
Unless he's really clean.

Don't read those magazines, dear,
They're all a load of trash;
You should think of better ways, dear,
To spend your hard-earned cash.

Those heels look awfully high, dear,
Your legs aren't fully grown.
Finish your conversation, dear,
I need to use the phone.

Tidy up that bedroom, dear,
It really is a tip.
If you sulk any more, dear,
You'll trip over your bottom lip.

Those posters on your wall, dear,
I find them rather crude;
It really isn't nice, dear,
To look at young men nude.

Stand up nice and straight, dear,
Don't ever slump or slouch.
Do homework at your desk, dear,
Not lying on the couch.

Turn off that awful noise, dear,
We can't hear ourselves think.
Open up a window, dear,
What is that dreadful stink?

Go and have a walk, dear,
The air will do you good.
Don't come in the house, dear,
Your shoes are covered in mud.

That film is just for adults, dear,
And life is never fair;
What everybody else does, dear,
Is neither here nor there.

Your language is atrocious, dear,
Your granny would be shocked;
Say that word again, dear,
And your income will be docked.

I know you think we're nagging, dear,
And really quite a bore;
You'll thank us when you're older, dear,
Don't slam the b***** door!

Their nagging really gets to me,
It causes so much strife;
They say it's for my own good, but
They're ruining my life!

An Nollaig

CRIOSTÓIR Ó FLATHARTA

Seo é an cur síos a rinne Mamaí dom ar an Nollaig chomh fada agus is cuimhin léi féin í:

Ní raibh mórán airgead acu ag an am, mar sin ní raibh an oiread sin cístí, milseán, brioscaí ná a lán rudaí eile fairsing acu. Dhéanadh Mamó cúpla cáca rísíní sa bhácús os cionn na tine oscailte. Is minic a bhíodh cuid mhaith den cháca ite nuair a thógtaí te as an mbácús é.

Bhíodh cearca, lachain nó géamha sa teach ag an am. Mharaíodh Mamó gé nó lacha nó cearc, b'fhéidir, agus bhíodh sí acu i gcomhair an dinnéir lá Nollag. Ba síos sa bhácús a chuirtí an ghé nó an lacha seo agus chuirtí anraith síos léi. Ní raibh aon chaint ar í a róstadh an t-am sin.

Thagadh Daidí na Nollag chuig na páistí agus ba bhronntanas amháin cosúil le gúna nua nó bróga nó bríste nó geansaí a thugadh sé dóibh. Bhíodh coinneal mhór dhearg ar lasadh i lár an bhoird oíche Nollag agus coinneal i ngach fuinneog chomh maith.

Théadh na daoine chuig an Aifreann de shiúl a gcos maidin lá Nollag. Bhíodh beagán maisiúcháin ar na tithe i gcomhair na Nollag cosúil le slám balún ar crochadh agus mar sin de. Bhíodh Mamó go maith ag marú cearc nó lachan, a dúirt mo mhamaí liom.

Bhíodh ciseog acu freisin ag an am sin le haghaidh na bhfataí a dhoirteadh amach uirthi. Is minic a rinne Daideo ciseog nua le haghaidh na Nollag agus bhíodh sí ag breathnú go deas i lár an bhoird.

Ní raibh an saol chomh maith an uair sin agus atá sé inniu, ach mar sin féin, bhí Mamaí agus iad ar fad sona sásta leis an Nollaig a bhíodh acu.

My Nana

ANNA TWOMEY

I love my Nana. She is small and plump and her hair is going grey. She is very agile for her age and she never stops working. Her green eyes twinkle when she sees me. I am her favourite grandchild, even though she also likes my three brothers.

Nana used to love sweet things, especially cream buns and clover-rocks (hard sweets). Now she is a diabetic and has to give them all up. She loves being outside, looking after her flowers. Her garden is magnificent. Her favourite flowers are roses. She also loves her dogs, cats, chickens and turkeys. The turkeys, however, are now all stuffed and gone where all good turkeys go! She feeds the dogs Pedigree Chum and Champ and potato skins. Her favourite dog is Des. She likes him best because he is always in a playful mood.

Nana wears Puma tracksuit pants around the house. When she is out in the yard, she wears big, strong boots and knitted hats. When she dresses up she puts on lipstick and powder and squirts on any perfume she can find.

At night she takes out her teeth and puts them into a cup with Correga Tabs. These tablets are white to clean her teeth. She looks very funny without her teeth.

Nana is a great cook. She makes me lovely stews and scrambled eggs. I also love the smell of her brown and white soda bread. It pirouettes in the kitchen air. The kitchen is always roasting hot. Nana loves putting down big fires with loads of turf, coal and sticks. Granda sweats in the kitchen while he reads the *North Cork News*.

My favourite place in the whole world is my Nana's house in Bally, even though I rather like my home in Millstreet too. Nana tells me stories of the threshing and of when she was a little girl. She never minds if I don't brush my hair properly or if I wear my clothes inside-out or jumbled up. She goes very easy brushing my hair when it is tangled.

Sometimes I sleep over in Bally. I sleep in Nana's bed. It is lovely and warm, with a fluffy duvet and a covered hot-water bottle for my feet. I could stay there forever. I love my Nana and I love making cards for such a 'special person'.

The Flood Disaster

C A R M E L   F A H Y

I remember looking down on the farmyard. All the animals were floating on the water, except for the few hens who cackled loudly as they all clustered together on the oak tree. I remember my little brother crying loudly and my mother rocking him softly from side to side, telling him that it would all be over soon. I could feel the cold hands of my father as he held me tightly in his arms. We sat on that rooftop for almost an hour.

It all began one terrible day. The rain poured down heavily. We could hear the harsh wind blowing strongly and the wooden gates of the byre banging. I couldn't believe how fast the storm was rising. My brother and I sat in the corner of the kitchen on the cold stone floor. We wondered when our parents would come back in from the farmyard. They had gone out to gather up all the animals and put them safely in their sheds. My mother was the first to come back. She told us that our father had gone to check the level of the river. Our mother tried to call our nearest neighbour, but the telephone lines were dead. Then she tried to turn on the cooker for some hot water for tea, but the electricity was out.

When our father came back we could hear him

talking to our mother. He was saying that the river would definitely flood over, but that it would hold out for at least another hour. He told her that the animals were all panic-stricken and that the roads leading to the river were flowing with muddy water from the rain. He had locked the stables, but I knew that they both knew the horses would easily kick the doors down. The chicken coop and the byre were both tightly locked. My mother looked at my father with wide eyes. She didn't say anything because she didn't want us to panic, even though she knew that we had already heard everything from our father.

It had been two days since we were able to move from the house. The water was seeping through the crack at the bottom of the door, even though there were about five large towels protecting it. The water level had now reached about a metre. Then, on the third day, it all happened. Just when we thought the worst was over, the river burst its banks. We could actually hear it, even though it was over half a mile away.

Soon enough we could see the swirling, muddy waters, twisting and turning their way up the narrow road. After about two minutes the whole farmyard was flooded. The water burst through all the sheds. The hens flew everywhere, until they finally perched themselves on the branches of the old oak tree. We could see the horses trying to reach for safety. Where, we didn't know. Only their heads could be seen as they waded through the water. The pigs were already dead, and we could see them floating on the water. The ducks were the only happy animals, swimming merrily on the water.

Our dad fetched the ladder which was folded up in the back room. He broke a hole in the window. All the water came rushing in. It stopped just as the level was reaching my knees. The water was freezing and muddy. My dad put the ladder outside the window and fixed it so that it just touched the top of the roof. My mum climbed out first and she brought my brother with her. Then it was my turn.

My father helped me out. Then my mum grabbed my hand and lifted me up. It wasn't long before my father came up.

We looked out over the countryside. It was one big, giant lake. We waited anxiously for help. My mother prayed loudly. We all hoped that rescue would come soon. We shivered with the cold, drenched to the skin. My father held me tightly in his cold, strong arms. We were marooned on that roof for about an hour. At last we could hear the noise of a helicopter. It soon came into sight. It hovered overhead for a minute or two before it finally became steady. The door of the helicopter slid back and out came a man tied onto a harness. He was lowered down slowly but surely. My mother gave out a huge sigh of relief. I thanked God so many times, over and over in my mind.

First the man took my brother and pulled him up. Then he reached for my hand. I grabbed it and held on tightly. My mother was next and finally my father. We were taken away to safety in the hospital of the nearest town. We were examined closely. The doctor gave my mother some tablets for my brother, because he had swallowed some dirty water while climbing out of the window. My mother was worried about where we were going to stay, but my father told us that he would telephone one of his friends who lived in the town and ask if we could stay for a while. He was a close friend of Dad's, so he

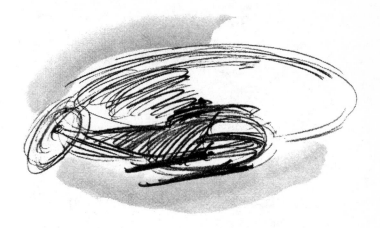

kindly insisted that we stay there until everything was cleared up.

News came through on the radio about three weeks later that the flooding was receding, and by the end of that week we were able to see our home, or what was left of it. We drove through the muddy roads to our house. The dead animals had already been disposed of. We looked at the farm. I could see sadness and anger in my father's eyes. He had been living here since he was born and his family had lived here for generations.

I was sad to see our house. The roof had actually fallen in. The floor was wet and muddy and it felt soft beneath our feet. I looked up at the broken window which we had climbed out of and I knew that I would never forget the day of the terrible flood that ruined my home forever.

Forest News

CLODAGH NÍ
CHEARBHAILL

FOREST NEWS

Volume 1, Issue 1   25 February 1998

OUR ON-THE-SPOT
REPORT:

I interviewed the mother of the 'ugly duckling', as the townspeople are calling him. All she would say was that it couldn't possibly be hers and that she was going to put an ad in our paper. She said that if that didn't work she would simply get rid of him.

MAIN ARTICLE

The big news in the forest is that the poor mother of six little ducklings has had an ugly one.

Having been a model this came as a very big shock – not only is it ugly but it's untalented.

NOTICES

FA Cup (Forest Animals) trials next Tuesday.
All welcome.

Duck found
Description: ugly and untalented.

Ask paper for information.

FOREST NEWS

Volume 1, Issue 2   26 February 1998

OUR ON-THE-SPOT
REPORT:

Today I interviewed one of the ugly duckling's brothers. He said that he agreed with his mother all the way. He also said that even if they had to pay someone to take him away they should do it. He said it was all the ugly duckling's fault that his mummy was sick.

MAIN ARTICLE

The mother of the ugly duckling fainted after one look at its first attempt to swim.

She was immediately rushed to the nearest hospital and is said to be in a stable condition, suffering only from shock.

NOTICES

Duck minder needed. Four bags of corn an hour.

FA Cup Team:

Ellie the Elephant
Billy the Goat
Mickey the Mouse
Ollie the Owl

FOREST NEWS

Volume 1, Issue 3   27 February 1998

OUR ON-THE-SPOT REPORT:

As the days have gone by the ugly duckling has become less ugly and more graceful. He has also started to change from his ugly brownish colour to a creamy white.

MAIN ARTICLE

The father of the ugly duckling has been found! It turns out that the ugly duckling is actually a swan!

What actually happened was that the mother of the swan went insane and thought she was a cuckoo. So, as all cuckoos do, she left her egg in somebody else's nest.

The father had been looking for days and was absolutely delighted to finally meet his son. They both say a big huge 'thank you' to the dear lady who took care of him.

Sceitimíní

MARY CASSERLEY

Sceitimíní Sceitimíní Sceitimíní.
Is maith liom an focal sin.
Tá gliondar orm.
Tá mo chosa ag léim.
Tá mo lámha ag damhsa.
Tá mo chroí ag gáire.
Sceitimíní Sceitimíní Sceitimíní.
Yippee Yippee!

Freak

A M I E   O ' D O N O G H U E

For me, crushes are not uncommon – heady, lustful feelings for absolute strangers which leave me elated, frustrated and depressed.

The boy in question becomes an icon, a huge, powerful demigod who can do no wrong. He becomes a daily visitor to both my dreams and daydreams – huge romantic extravaganzas, usually involving champagne, roses and violins.

My friends and I are all terrible flirts. I have no problem admitting to that, it's perfectly respectable. Every lunchtime, without fail, we all stream out into the park across the road, giddy with anticipation.

Lately though, I have found myself tiring of this. It's the same all the time. Boys are all the same, a tiny bit of flattery and they never shut up about themselves. Scratch any male and you will always find an enormous ego, a strange compulsion to talk about sports and a proud broadcast of his drinking plans for the weekend. Oh, the thrill.

Now, I've never admitted this to anyone, but I have developed the most disturbingly enormous crush on someone amazing. He has become my dream visitor, but a much more troublesome one than usual.

I am hopelessly infatuated with him – I have palpitations every time I see him, for God's sake. However, there is just one enormous, gaping, towering problem: he's different, and I adore him for it.

He's an outsider – a freak, a spacer, a weirdo, a retard (a god?). He doesn't look, dress or think like the crowd and the worst thing is he's proud of it.

I wish people weren't so scared. I'm not sure why he's looked down upon, but it seems the only reason is because he has the courage and individuality to stand out. It makes me so frustrated sometimes – I'd be sitting in the park, giggling inanely at some forgettable boy, all the time stealing glances at my freak, wishing I could talk to him, just longing to start up a conversation.

He looks like he would possibly have something more interesting to talk about than the 'class' match the other day, or how himself and the lads got so utterly 'locked' the other night that they smashed all the factory windows. Totally lethal lad, way cool boy, completely juvenile and amazingly mind-numbingly boring man, but hey, I'll just smile vapidly, witter on about what a man you are and successfully hide the fact that I have a mind. An opinion, even.

Sometimes I get a mad urge to actually ask a question rather than just listen: 'So tell me, Michael, what are your opinions (Opinions? Ha! That's a good one) on gay marriage? Abortion? Women's rights? Pollution? Animal testing? Do you believe in life after death? Buddhism? Hypnotism? Reincarnation? Extra-terrestrial life? Voodoo? The Loch Ness Monster?'

I can just picture the look of sheer terror (picture a rabbit caught in headlights), followed by the derisive curl of his lip. He'd nudge a friend and they'd whisper in shocked tones about my 'coming out' as a complete and utter spacer.

But no, I'd never do anything that wild – such rebellious antics are not socially acceptable. My life always has and probably always will follow the dictates of society.

I should really give up on my freak, because even if he liked me back I wouldn't do a thing about it. I wouldn't even allow myself to be seen talking to him, so I'll just have to have pseudo-real conversations with him in my dreams, where he remains a disturbing and most troublesome visitor.

A voice in my head reproaches me for my narrow-mindedness and prejudice, but I say that I'm better safe than sorry.

Mo Chaipín

CLÍODHNA McCAUGHEY

Mo chaipín ar mo cheann,
Dearg agus bán,
Mo chaipín ar mo cheann,
Is mé ag canadh amhrán!

Mo chaipín ar mo cheann,
Glas agus dubh,
Mo chaipín ar mo cheann,
Is mé ag ithe uibhe!

Mo chaipín ar mo cheann,
Gorm agus buí,
Mo chaipín ar mo cheann,
Is mé i mo luí!

The Haunted House

L A U R A   E G A N

Once upon a time there lived a king, a queen and a princess. One winter's night a witch cast a spell on their castle. The spell was that they would all die. Next day they all died. The castle was not touched for many years because it became haunted.

It had a dungeon with lots of snakes, big spiders and rats. It also had a graveyard for a front garden. The king, the queen and the princess haunted anyone who came near the castle, especially builders.

The only way to break the spell was for a prince to spring-clean the castle, but no-one knew that that was the way. If the spell was broken the townspeople would have a king, a queen and a princess to rule the land again.

One day a prince was in town. He spotted the castle and went up to the door and knocked on it. It opened by itself. He went in. It started to rain and the prince decided he could not go home in that rain. So he had to stay there that night. There were cobwebs everywhere. Being a tidy person, he cleaned the whole castle from top to bottom. It was spotless but the spell was not broken because there was still the dungeon. The prince didn't know there

was a dungeon and never found out for a week.

The next week he went home to his own castle. He asked his mum and dad to move to the other castle. They said, 'Okay, dear.' The next day they moved in. They thought it was a lovely castle, better than their old one, but things were a bit strange. They didn't mind though. Sometimes they would get a shiver down their backs, but only sometimes. They lived there for a year and they still didn't know about the dungeon.

One day the prince found a small door in the castle. He opened it and there, inside, were lots and lots of big spiders, rats and snakes. His mum was looking for him. She looked in the door and screamed, because she hated spiders and rats and snakes. She said, 'Get them out of the castle now.' The prince just closed the door and did nothing. The spell was still not broken because he had just closed the door and he hadn't taken the spiders, rats and snakes out.

One day his mum found out that he hadn't taken the snakes and other things out. She ordered him to do so. So he quickly took the snakes, rats and spiders out. Suddenly the spell was broken.

There was a flash of lightning and a crash of thunder, and little stars fell to the ground, and then there was a big puff of smoke. There stood the king, the queen and the princess.

The minute the princess saw the prince she fell in

love with him and the prince fell in love with her. They decided to get married and have children. They had a big wedding.

The king and queen said that the other king and queen could move in and live with them as long as they wanted to, especially now that their son was married and happily so.

Space

RUAIDHRÍ OISÍN GIBLIN

Space is a place,
A big mystery case,
Where stars
Like Mars
Are big and dark;
Nobody called Clark.

Aliens with no nose
And 336 toes;
Scientists sitting beside
Telescopes,
Hoping to find horoscopes.

Stars which light the sky
As spaceships go zooming by,
Dull and grey,
Going far and away;
Probes
Circumnavigating globes,
Sending back scenes,
Hoping to find greens.

Growing plants in space!
Could that be what we face?

Space,
What a place.

Contributors

Puppy by Gregory Mimnagh-Dunne. Gregory is 6 years old, lives in Mullingar, Co Westmeath, and goes to Presentation Convent Junior School in Mullingar.

Pauli the Python by Lara Cassidy. Lara is 6 years old. She lives in Ballinasloe, Co Galway, and goes to Scoil Mhuire in Ballinasloe.

The Wrong Parcel by Jenny McCarthy. Jenny is $10\frac{1}{2}$ years old, lives in Clonmel, Co Tipperary, and attends Powerstown National School in Clonmel.

On the Moon by Killian Donovan. Killian is 6 years old and lives in Kilgobbin Road in Dublin. He goes to Our Lady of the Wayside National School in Kilternan, Co Dublin.

Hippopotamalla by Bríd Faulkner. Bríd is 11 years old, lives in Blackrock, Co Dublin, and goes to Loreto Primary School in Dalkey, Co Dublin.

My Sisters by Conall McNamara. Conall is 11 years old. He lives in Achill Sound, Achill Island, and goes to Tonragee National School on Achill.

Lost by Suzanne Carter. Suzanne is 11 years old and lives in Ard-na-Gréine in Dublin. She goes to Sutton Park School in Sutton, Dublin.

The Secret by Karen Clarke. Karen is 10 years old, lives in Navan, Co Meath, and goes to Our Lady of Mercy Primary School in Kells, Co Meath.

Tigger and Goldie by Laura Barriscale. Laura is 7 years old, lives in Swords, Co Dublin, and goes to Pope John Paul II National School in Malahide, Co Dublin.

Ted by Jennifer Henry. Jennifer is 6 years old. She lives in Finglas West in Dublin and goes to St Brigid's National School in Finglas West.

Domhnach is Dálach by Seán Ó Loingsigh. Seán is 13 years old, lives in Carlow, and goes to Gaelcholáiste Cheatharlach, Carlow.

The Big Spaceship by Michael Reidy. Michael is 9 years old. He lives in Castletown, Co Kildare, and goes to Scoil na Mainistreach in Celbridge, Co Kildare.

Jackpot by Maria Meally. Maria is 12 years old, lives in Moycullen, Co Galway, and goes to Scoil Chaitríona in Renmore, Galway.

Lá Mór a Bhí Agam by Páraic Ó hÉannraich. Páraic is 9 years old. He lives in An Caisleáin Nua, Co Dublin, and goes to Scoil Chrónáin in Rath Cúil, Co Dublin.

Fireworks by Sinéad Forde. Sinéad is 10 years old and lives in Kilcullen, Co Kildare. She attends Blessington No.1 School in Blessington, Co Wicklow.

A Day in the Life of My Dog! by Orla Loughman. Orla is 10 years old, lives in Milltown in Dublin and goes to Presentation Primary School in Terenure, Dublin.

The Purr-fect Catwalk by Steven Markey. Steven is 12 years old, lives in Blackrock, Co Louth, and goes to St Oliver Plunkett's National School in Blackrock.

Uaigneas by Mairéad Ní Choistealbha. Mairéad is 14 years old, lives in Baile na hAbhann, Co Galway, and goes to Coláiste Chroí Mhuire in An Spidéal, Co Galway.

Dinosaur Land by Kevin O'Regan. Kevin is 5 years old. He lives in Arklow, Co Wicklow, and goes to St Joseph's National School in Arklow.

The Kill by Gail Cummins. Gail is 12 years old, lives in Kildare, Co Kildare, and attends Scoil Mhuire, Newbridge, Co Kildare.

Rampaging Rimmer by James Duff. James is 10 ¾ years old. He lives in Skerries, Co Dublin, and goes to school in Skerries.

If I had Three Wishes by Mark O'Regan. Mark is 10 years old, lives in Montenotte in Cork and goes to St Patrick's Boys' National School in Cork.

Childhood Pastimes by Aislinn Flaherty. Aislinn is 12 years old. She lives in Tuam, Co Galway, and goes to Presentation Primary School in Tuam.

No Exit by Aoife Cahill. Aoife is 13 years old, lives in Mallow, Co Cork, and goes to Coláiste an Chroí Naofa in Carraig na bhFear, Co Cork.

Ag Fanacht by Maria Ní Dhuinnín. Maria is 10 years old, lives in Macroom, Co Cork, and goes to S.N. Lachtain Naofa in Macroom.

The Intruder by Audrey Walsh. Audrey is 8 years old and lives in Dundalk, Co Louth. She goes to Tallanstown National School in Dundalk.

I Remember by Tadhg Ó Broin. Tadhg is 14 years old. He lives in Bray, Co Wicklow, and goes to Coláiste Eoin, Baile an Bhóthair, Dublin.

Puddin by Michael Callery. Michael is 9 years old, lives in Elphin, Co Roscommon, and goes to Abbey Cartron National School in Elphin.

One of those Days by *Andrea Bonnie. Andrea is 12 years old, lives in Santry in Dublin and goes to Holy Child Senior Girls' National School in Whitehall, Dublin.*

Inspiration by *Sorcha McDonagh. Sorcha is 9 years old. She lives in Ranelagh in Dublin and goes to St Mary's National School in Donnybrook, Dublin.*

The Puca by *Peter Martin. Peter is 11 years old and lives in Strandhill, Co Sligo. He goes to Scoil Asicus in Strandhill.*

An Turas by *Nóríde Ní Mhuimhneacháin. Nóríde is 9 years old, lives in Macroom, Co Cork, and goes to S.N. Lachtain Naofa in Macroom.*

Macs 'n' Milkshakes by *Michelle McDaid. Michelle is 12 years old, lives in Carndonagh, Co Donegal, and goes to St Brigid's National School in Carndonagh.*

My Collection of Colours by *Aileen Armstrong. Aileen is 14 years old, lives in Rosses Point, Co Sligo, and goes to Ursuline College in Finisklin, Sligo.*

An Bád Bán, *Eimear O'Loughlin. Eímear is 16 years old and lives in Maddoxtown, Co Kilkenny. She goes to Loreto Secondary School, Granges Road, Co Kilkenny.*

A Week in My Life – a Witch's Story by *Laura Power. Laura is 11 years old. She lives in Taylor's Hill, Galway, and goes to Scoil Íde in Salthill, Galway.*

Nothing to Do with Fish … by *Val Nolan (Jnr.) Val is 15 years old, lives in Ardagh, Co Limerick, and goes to Scoil Mhuire agus Íde in Newcastle West, Co Limerick.*

Inis Oirr by *Diarmaid Ó hAlmhain. Diarmaid is 9 years old. He lives on Inis Oirr, Co Galway, and goes to Scoil Chaomháin, Inis Oirr, Co Galway.*

The Spell that Went Wrong by *Fergus Monnelly. Fergus is almost 10 years old. He lives in Foxrock, Dublin, and goes to St Patrick's B.N.S. in Blackrock, Co Dublin.*

An Muicín Dána by *Colm Ó Cuinn. Colm is 10 years old, lives in Leitir Móir, Co Galway, and goes to Scoil Rónán in Leitir Móir.*

A Normal Day by *Sinéad Campbell. Sinéad is 11 years old and lives in Clonmel, Co Tipperary. She goes to Scoil Mhuire na nAingeal in Clonmel.*

Change by *John Hoskin. John is 12 years old, lives in Clonakilty, Co Cork, and goes to school in Bandon, Co Cork.*

Alone by Clare Holohan. Clare is 13 years old. She lives in Blackrock, Co Dublin, and attends Loreto Abbey in Dalkey, Co Dublin.

For Your Own Good by Ellie Fry. Ellie is 15 years old and lives in Rathfarnham in Dublin. She goes to The High School in Rathgar, Dublin.

An Nollaig by Criostóir Ó Flatharta. Criostóir is 12 years old. He lives in Leitir Mór, Co Galway, and goes to Scoil Bhríde in Leitir Mór.

My Nana by Anna Twomey. Anna is 10 years old, lives in Millstreet, Co Cork, and goes to Presentation Convent in Millstreet.

The Flood Disaster by Carmel Fahy. Carmel is 12 years old, lives in Croom, Co Limerick, and goes to school in Croom.

Forest News by Clodagh Ní Chearbhaill. Clodagh is 11 years old, lives in Bray, Co Wicklow, and attends St Patrick's National School in Bray.

Sceitimíní by Mary Casserley. Mary is 8 years old, lives in Elphin, Co Roscommon, and goes to Abbey Cartron National School in Elphin.

Freak by Amie O'Donoghue. Amie is 14 years old and lives in Dungourney, Co Cork. She goes to St Mary's High School in Midleton, Co Cork.

Mo Chaipín by Clíodhna McCaughey. Clíodhna is 7 years old, lives in Churchtown in Dublin and goes to Scoil Naithí in Ballinteer, Dublin.

The Haunted House by Laura Egan. Laura is 9 years old. She lives in Bray, Co Wicklow, and goes to Ravenswell National School in Bray.

Space by Ruaidhrí Oisín Giblin. Ruaidhrí is 10 years old and lives in Glasnevin, Dublin. He goes to St Patrick's Boys' National School in Drumcondra, Dublin.

Note: The above information is correct at time of submission.

Other books from
THE O'BRIEN PRESS

THE BLUE HORSE
Winner Bisto Book of the Year Overall Award (1993)
When their caravan burns down, Katie's family must move to live in a house on a new estate. But for Katie, this means trouble. Is she strong enough to deal with the new situation?

Paperback £3.99/$6.95

HORSE THIEF
Hugh Galt
Rory's beloved old mare disappears. Then three girls discover a racehorse kidnapped and held for ransom near their home. These two stories interweave into a nail-biting story, full of action and thrills.

Paperback £3.99/$6.95

MISSING SISTERS
Gregory Maguire
In a fire in a holiday home, Alice's favourite nun is injured and disappears to hospital. Back at the orphanage, Alice is faced with difficult choices, then a surprise enters her life when she meets a girl called Miami.

Paperback £3.99

From Gerard Whelan

THE GUNS OF EASTER

Winner Bisto Book of the Year Eilís Dillon Award 1997

Winner Bisto Book of the Year Merit Award 1997

It is 1916: from the poverty of the Dublin slums twelve-year-old Jimmy Conway sees the war in Europe as glorious, and loves the British Army for which his father is fighting. But when war comes to his own streets, Jimmy's loyalties are divided. Looking for food for his family, Jimmy crosses the city avoiding the shooting, weaving through army patrols, hoping to make it home before curfew.

Paperback £4.99/$6.95

A WINTER OF SPIES

Eleven-year-old Sarah wants to be part of the rebellion in Dublin in 1920. She doesn't realise that her family are an important part of Michael Collins's spy ring, and her actions endanger them all. Sequel to the award-winning *The Guns of Easter*.

Paperback £4.99/$7.95

DREAM INVADER

Winner Bisto Book of the Year Overall Award 1998

When Saskia goes to stay with her uncle and aunt she finds them worried about her little cousin Simon, who is having terrible dreams. Something strange is definitely going on. Then an old woman enters the scene. The forces of good and evil fight for control over the child while Saskia watches the horrible events unfold ...

Paperback £4.50/$7.95

From Siobhán Parkinson

FOUR KIDS, THREE CATS, TWO COWS, ONE WITCH (maybe)

Winner Bisto Book of the Year Merit Award 1998

Beverly, Elizabeth, Kevin, Gerard and his cat visit the mysterious Lady Island, expecting some adventure and a little danger. But nothing prepares them for their encounter with the strange inhabitant of the island.

Paperback £4.50/$6.95

Sisters ... No Way!

Winner Bisto Book of the Year Overall Award 1997

Cindy does NOT want her Dad to remarry after her mother's death – especially not Ashling's mum. No way do these two want to become sisters! Two diaries record the events, from two very different teenagers. A *flipper* book, this story deals with teenage life in an amusing and unusual way.

Paperback £4.50/$7.95

THE MOON KING

Ricky's new foster home is full of sunshine and laughter and children of all ages. But Ricky doesn't know how to be part of the family and withdraws to a magical chair in the attic, which becomes his throne. He becomes the Moon King and begins to open up and trust again, but there is opposition and jealousy to overcome before he can find real happiness and friendship.

Paperback £4.99/$7.95

HORSE THIEF
Hugh Galt

Rory's beloved old mare disappears. Then three girls discover a racehorse kidnapped and held for ransom near their home. These two stories interweave into a nail-biting story, full of action and thrills.

Paperback £3.99/$6.95

MISSING SISTERS
Gregory Maguire

In a fire in a holiday home, Alice's favourite nun is injured and disappears to hospital. Back at the orphanage, Alice is faced with difficult choices, then a surprise enters her life when she meets a girl called Miami.

Paperback £3.99

Send for our full colour catalogue

ORDER FORM

Please send me the books as marked

I enclose cheque/postal order for £ . . . . (+£1.00 P&P per title)

OR please charge my credit card ___ Access/Mastercard ___ Visa

Card Number __ __ __ __   __ __ __ __   __ __ __ __   __ __ __ __

Expiry Date _____ / _____

Name. . . . . Tel: . . . .

Address . . . .

. . . .

Please send orders to : THE O'BRIEN PRESS, 20 Victoria Road, Dublin 6.

Tel: +353 1 4923333 Fax: + 353 1 4922777 email: books@obrien.ie

Internet:http://www.obrien.ie